SURVIVAL

LIFE AND ART OF THE ALASKAN ESKIMO

46-75

SURVIVAL

LIFE AND ART OF THE ALASKAN ESKIMO

BARBARA LIPTON
Guest Curator

Introduction by
DR. FROELICH RAINEY

Annotated Bibliography by
ALLAN CHAPMAN

THE NEWARK MUSEUM
Newark, New Jersey

THE AMERICAN FEDERATION OF ARTS
New York, New York

The publication and the exhibition have been made possible
with the support of the National Endowment for the Humanities

Front Cover:
Hunter on Norton Sound
Nome, 1974

Back Cover:
Butchering a Seal
Gambell, St. Lawrence Island, 1975

Frontispiece:
177. MASK
Painted wood depicting a wolf's face with open mouth;
separately carved teeth and ears.
8½" (21.7 cm.) high
c. 1935
Kuskokwim River
Newark Museum; 38.343 a-c
The wolf mask represented hunting prowess for
all the people.

730027

Design by Leon Auerbach

Front and back covers and photographs of Alaska
by Barbara Lipton
© Barbara Lipton 1977

All objects photographed by Bob Hanson, New York,
except for Mask p. 32

Photograph of Mask p. 32 courtesy of the
University of Alaska Museum, Fairbanks

Printed by Morgan Press Inc., Dobbs Ferry, New York

Typography by Unbekant Typo, Inc., New York

© The Newark Museum 1977

Library of Congress Catalog Card Number: 76-53613
ISBN: 0-87100-121-7

The Newark Museum Association
43-49 Washington Street
Newark, New Jersey 07101

The American Federation of Arts
41 East 65th Street
New York, New York 10021

Published in cooperation with:
Morgan and Morgan, Inc.
145 Palisade Street
Dobbs Ferry, New York 10522

LETTER FROM THE GOVERNOR OF ALASKA

I am very pleased that the Newark Museum has seen fit to provide an exhibition entitled *Survival: Life and Art of the Alaskan Eskimo* as part of its program. Too often a stereotyped depiction of the Alaskan Eskimo has been placed before the public by fiction writers and movie scripters, and it is indeed a pleasure to have the Eskimo way of life, their art, and handicraft displayed in this most professional manner.

This exhibition shows the adaptation of the Alaskan Eskimo to an often hostile and difficult environment from pre-historic times to the period of contact with the white man, to the present day when the survival of his cultural identity is at stake in a rapidly changing world in Alaska. It emphasizes the beauty and utility of the Eskimo's creations and includes artifacts, tools and utensils, clothing, masks, ivory carvings, paintings, prints and photographs.

The director and staff of the Newark Museum and the contributors to this exhibition are to be commended for their professional presentation of this exhibit. I know that it will create a lasting impression upon those who view through this exhibit the diversified and rich culture of the Alaskan Eskimo.

Sincerely,

JAY S. HAMMOND
Governor
State of Alaska

FOREWORD

The Newark Museum and The American Federation of Arts are pleased to sponsor this exhibition presenting the rich and varied art and culture of Alaskan Eskimos from prehistoric times to the present day. The Newark Museum's collection of Eskimo objects, many of which have not been shown previously, form the nucleus of this show. In addition, other specimens have been borrowed from public and private collections in Alaska and the Lower 48 States in order better to illustrate the differences and similarities in the ancient and contemporary lives of these Native Americans.

The show has been organized by Barbara Lipton as Guest Curator and Project Director, with the assistance of Anne Spencer, Curator of the Ethnological Collection of The Newark Museum. Mrs. Lipton has traveled extensively in Alaska and is well acquainted personally with many of the state's artists and government leaders, who have cooperated with her in the planning. She has provided a background essay for this book on the major themes covered by the exhibition to increase further the enjoyment and understanding of this rare material.

We wish to express our great appreciation to the National Endowment for the Humanities for their generous assistance in making this exhibition and publication possible.

SAMUEL C. MILLER
Director
The Newark Museum

WILDER GREEN
Director
The American Federation of Arts

ACKNOWLEDGMENTS

We should like to express our appreciation to Governor Jay Hammond of Alaska for his statement of support.

We should also like to extend our thanks to the museums which have contributed objects from their collections: The University of Alaska Museum, Fairbanks; The Alaska State Museum, Juneau; The Anchorage Museum of Historical and Fine Arts; The Visual Arts Center, Anchorage; The Field Museum of Natural History, Chicago; The Peabody Museum of Archaeology and Ethnology, Harvard University, Cambridge; The Peabody Museum of Salem; The University Museum, Philadelphia; The Haffenreffer Museum, Brown University, Bristol, R.I.; The National Museum of Natural History, Smithsonian Institution, Washington, D.C.; The East Hampton Town Marine Museum, Amagansett, N.Y.; and The American Museum of Natural History, New York. We also wish to express our appreciation to the personnel of the above-mentioned museums for their courteous and helpful assistance.

We are very grateful to Mr. and Mrs. Douglas D. Anderson for artifacts and for photographs taken in the Kobuk and Selawik River regions and at Onion Portage; to Mrs. Diana Tillion who has generously lent us two of her watercolor paintings; to the National Park Service, U.S. Department of the Interior, for photographs from their exhibit, "Alaska: The Great Land"; to BP Alaska for photographs of Prudhoe Bay and to the private lenders to the exhibition who wish to remain anonymous.

To Dr. Froelich Rainey, Consultant to the exhibition, our sincerest thanks for his interest, assistance and advice, as well as the Introduction to this catalog. To Allan Chapman, Bibliographic Consultant to the exhibition, our appreciation for the scholarly, annotated bibliography he has prepared. To Larry Ahvakana, my personal thanks for allowing me to record our conversation. To Sandra Barz and Donna Ferrari, our thanks for their help in compiling the list of other museums with important Eskimo collections.

I should especially like to convey my warmest thanks to my many friends in Alaska who have welcomed me and shared a portion of their lives and their thoughts with me over the years.

BARBARA LIPTON
Guest Curator

CONTENTS

"SURVIVAL: LIFE AND ART OF THE ALASKAN ESKIMO", explores a new purpose and a new point of view in the use of museums and their collections.

The idea and much of the execution comes from Barbara Lipton. She does not have "a message" but with objects, pictures and statements presents a human situation touching upon all our lives. This is the story of a unique people in the crisis of rapid change which concludes with a question about the future— a question we all face. Eskimos are no longer the exotic, isolated, strange and primitive people as conceived by outsiders a generation ago, but a vital, contemporary people who make up a substantive part of the population in one of the fifty states. Their environment and their history may seem strange to most of us but their life problems and their adjustments to the crescendo of technological and social change are a contemporary human condition familiar to all of us.

Eskimos speak a language which does not relate to any other language in the world. They appeared in the Arctic at least 2,000 years ago and perhaps more than 6,000 years ago (depending upon what theory one accepts) but we do know that some of their villages are as old as Rome. There are remains of 2,000-year old villages on the northern tip of Greenland—farther north than any people live today.

Looking in from the outside it would seem that the Eskimo today, like most distinctive ethnic or national groups of people everywhere, are now, more than they were a decade ago, concerned with preserving their language, customs, beliefs, and world-view even though they have become integrated into the contemporary culture, social system, and political life of the general population of the country. Certainly there is nothing unique about this—the same goes for Poles, Latvians, Italians, or Irish. But, probably, Alaskan Eskimos have been so recently studied by anthropologists and archaeologists as subjects of "scientific research" that they resent more than most people the attitude of outsiders who have studied their history and customs as something rare and esoteric.

I understand and sympathize with the attitude of some contemporary Eskimo leaders derogatory to outside anthropologists and archaeologists. Already in 1940, while living, hunting, and fighting (family quarrels) with the people at Point Hope, Alaska, I had begun to wonder about my own presumption at recording "native" beliefs and customs. We anthropologists, of course, are not really as bad as we are now made out to be in Alaska but perhaps there still remains unconsciously among us a residue of the self-centered 19th century theory of recording and interpreting the ideas of strange and non-European people around the world in terms of our own beliefs, ideas, and preconceptions.

The Arctic I knew in the 1930's is long since gone. Then we traveled by dog team, river boat, trading schooner, umiak, or on foot, hunted for our own food with the Eskimos, and lived the slowly measured time of the changing seasons, the movements of pack ice, and the migrations of caribou, fish, and sea mammals—what has been described as the "cozy life" of the Arctic winter as seen from the "inside" rather than the "outside." Change has been rapid since the Second World War but the pace is dramatically accelerated by the Alaska Native Claims Settlement Act of 1971 which has given the Alaskan Eskimos, Indians, and Aleuts nearly 1 billion dollars and 40 million acres of land. What happens in an Eskimo village of a few hundred people when they suddenly have millions to spend? Hotels, apartment buildings, and houses pre-fabricated and shipped from Seattle, native industries and new airports rising on the tundra are incredible, but a reality. Now there may be as many as three snowmobiles to one family and the increasingly rare dog teams are used for sport racing!

An article in the New York Times speaks of a graffiti scribbled on a wall at Bethel, Alaska: "Time is what keeps everything from happening at once," and comments that "Bethel has become more and more the captive of the urgent kind of 20th century time that snaps ceaselessly at the heels of modern society." In Alaska these days everything "is happening at once." There the pace of technological and social change is accentuated to the point where we may see in a stereoscopic vision the basic human situation developing all over the world. Objects presented in a museum exhibition do not speak, but, as presented here, perhaps a work of art, a tool, a photograph, a statement, will evoke a chain of thought, a flash of comprehension, or meditation about human events that are crucial to all of us. This study of the Eskimos represents a moment in time and can have no conclusion, but I hope it achieves a better understanding of the only people who have created a successful and durable culture on Alaska's Arctic shores, and of what is now happening to them.

FROELICH RAINEY
July 1976

CHRONOLOGICAL CHART OF ALASKAN ARCTIC CULTURES

	ST. LAWRENCE ISLAND	NORTH AND WEST ALASKAN COAST	INTERIOR ALASKA KOBUK AREA
	RECENT ESKIMO CULTURE		
1750 A.D.			
	Recent Prehistoric	Recent Prehistoric Tigara	
1500 A.D.			
	Punuk	Western Thule	Arctic Woodland Eskimo
1000 A.D.			
		Birnirk	
500 A.D.	Old Bering Sea		
		Ipiutak Near Ipiutak	Norton/Ipiutak
0	Okvik	Norton	
500 B.C.			
		Choris	Choris
1000 B.C.			
1500 B.C.			
2000 B.C.			
		Denbigh Flint Complex	Denbigh Flint Complex
2500 B.C.			
			Palisades Complex
3000 B.C.			
		Trail Creek	Kobuk Complex
6000 B.C.			Akmak Complex

(Dates are approximate)

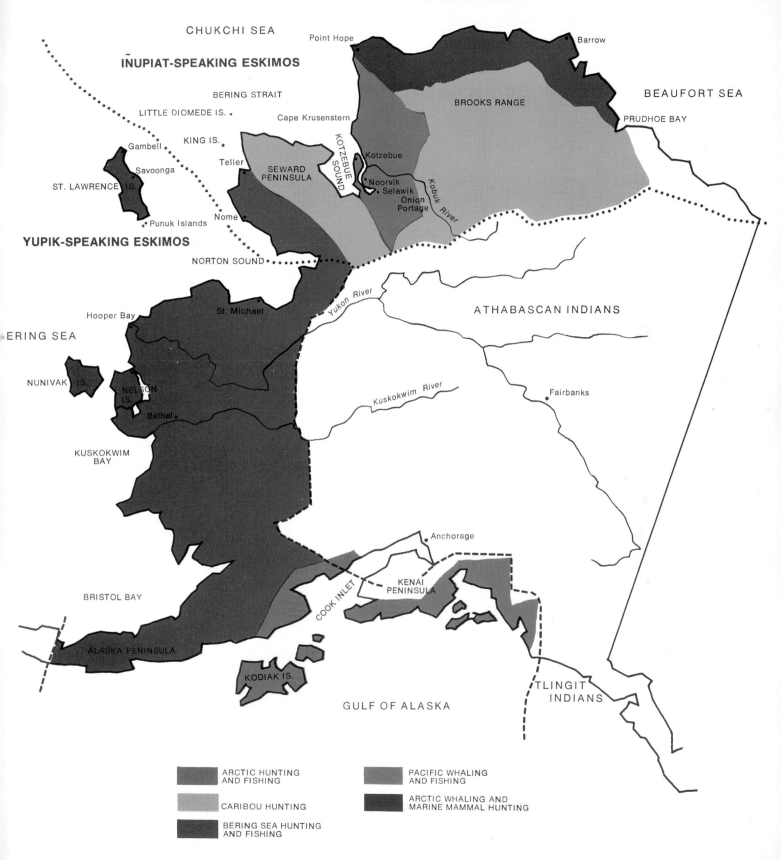

ARCTIC OCEAN

CHUKCHI SEA

ÑUPIAT-SPEAKING ESKIMOS

BERING STRAIT

LITTLE DIOMEDE IS.

KING IS.

Gambell

Savoonga

ST. LAWRENCE IS.

Punuk Islands

YUPIK-SPEAKING ESKIMOS

Point Hope

Barrow

BEAUFORT SEA

BROOKS RANGE

Cape Krusenstern

PRUDHOE BAY

Teller

SEWARD
PENINSULA

Kotzebue

KOTZEBUE SOUND

Noorvik
Selawik
Onion
Portage

Kobuk River

Nome

NORTON SOUND

Yukon River

ATHABASCAN INDIANS

Hooper Bay

St. Michael

ERING SEA

BERING SEA

NUNIVAK IS.

NELSON
IS.

Bethel

Kuskokwim River

Fairbanks

KUSKOKWIM
BAY

Anchorage

KENAI
PENINSULA

BRISTOL BAY

COOK INLET

ALASKA PENINSULA

KODIAK IS.

TLINGIT
INDIANS

GULF OF ALASKA

ARCTIC HUNTING
AND FISHING

PACIFIC WHALING
AND FISHING

CARIBOU HUNTING

ARCTIC WHALING AND
MARINE MAMMAL HUNTING

BERING SEA HUNTING
AND FISHING

49 KILLER WHALE
Walrus ivory with black engraving
6″ (15.2 cm.) long
Peter Mayac (c. 1908-   )
1973
Collection on loan to
The Newark Museum

*This exquisitely carved and engraved
whale expresses enormous vitality
despite its small size.*

SURVIVAL: LIFE AND ART OF THE ALASKAN ESKIMO

Introduction

The theme is SURVIVAL:

Survival of the Alaskan Eskimo people in a difficult and often hostile environment, one of the most forbidding on this planet;

Survival of a culture and a continuing way of life, lasting over thousands of years into the present day;

And now, the threat to survival of this ancient people and their traditional patterns from the impact of a modern society that is rapidly encroaching upon even the most remote regions of Alaska.

What does it mean to be an Eskimo? To physical anthropologists, an Eskimo is a distinct sub-species of the Mongoloid race with physical characteristics linking him most closely with peoples of northeastern Asia. To linguists, an Eskimo is someone who speaks one of the unique Eskimo languages or dialects. To an Eskimo, it means to live following the historical traditions of his ancestors—in the way he gets his food; in his feelings of physical and spiritual kinship with the land and the people and the animals around him; and in expressing himself in his own tongue and through the ancient ritualistic dances and songs.

Each of these perspectives of the Eskimo is, however, rapidly changing. With the advent of the white man in ever larger numbers, intermarriage and children of mixed blood have become increasingly frequent. White-administered public schools and U.S. Government agencies use English for instruction and communication, and English (although not always spoken with great fluency or ease) has become the first language of many younger Eskimos. Some retain little of their ancestral tongue. Christianity has supplanted the old beliefs in a world of spirits and the ancient ceremonial forms. And from the intrusion of an industrial society with its money economy, the Eskimo's subsistence patterns—formerly based on hunting and fishing and living off the land—have become more and more divergent from those of his forefathers. Today, continuity and conflict are interwoven in the fabric of Eskimo existence. The Eskimo will affirm with pride that he is an Eskimo, but increasingly the meaning of "Eskimo" becomes harder to define.

It is generally accepted by scientists that the first peoples came to the American continent from Asia by way of the Western Arctic perhaps as long ago as 30,000 years or more. There were successive waves of migration in prehistoric times as the seas lowered and rose, and the first men spread largely south and east. Some of the early migrators, however, remained in the northerly regions (now Alaska) which were at one time clear of glaciers but cut off from the rest of the American continent by huge ice fields. Although recent archaeological explorations in interior Alaska have definitely established the presence of man as early as 6,500 B. C. (and possibly as early as 13,000

B. C.),[1] the direct precursors of present-day Eskimos—that is, those early people who developed tools and cultural patterns clearly associated with an Eskimo way of life— are identifiable since perhaps 2,500 B. C. (It is possible that further location and excavation of old inhabited sites may push that date back even further.)

Although they have many similar features, the various Eskimo cultures that have evolved from these early inhabitants are not the same. From Alaska, the cradle of all Eskimo civilization in the New World, Eskimo people spread across the entire Polar regions of the northern hemisphere. They have in common what is basically the same language, although there are variations in dialect. They also share similar patterns of adaptation to the environment—in their hunting and fishing techniques, in their clothing and shelter, and in their perception of life.

The most northerly group, who are Iñupiat-speaking Eskimos, lives in the area from roughly north of Norton Sound in western Alaska throughout Arctic Canada and parts of Greenland.

Another large Eskimo group lives along the coastal regions of southwest and southern Alaska and in the delta formed by the Yukon and Kuskokwim Rivers. They speak Yupik, a different form of the Eskimo language. These southern Alaskan Eskimos also include the peoples of St. Lawrence Island in the Bering Sea, most of whose closest ancestors came from Siberia and who speak a form of Siberian Yupik. It is interesting that an Alaskan Iñupiat speaker can more readily understand an Eskimo from Greenland many thousands of miles away than he can a Yupik speaker who may be separated from him by only a short distance.

Alaskan Eskimos may also be further distinguished by their primary source of food supply. There are inland Eskimos who include both caribou-hunting, tundra dwellers and river-fishing peoples. And there are the coastal dwellers who are primarily sea-mammal hunters. The ways the various Eskimos wrested their living from these disparate environments contributed to shaping the differing cultural forms that emerged over a period of time.

Survival in a Hostile Environment

The physical characteristics of the land they occupy have always played a central role in the Eskimos' struggle for survival. The harsh northern climate, and with it the flora and fauna, varies to a considerable extent even within Alaska. Above the Arctic Circle, from the Canadian border in the east, through Barrow and Point Hope in the north, to Kotzebue on the west coast and to the Brooks Range in the interior, the land is a frigid semi-desert. There is little annual precipitation, and that largely in the form of snow. Winter temperatures can drop to 30° or 40° below zero on the coast and lower in the interior. Almost continual fierce winds make the temperatures seem even colder. No trees grow and there is only sparse vegetation and grasses on the tundra. Long hours of darkness prevail in winter. During spring and summer, however, the days are long and the temperatures can climb to 50° or more on the coast and much higher in the interior.

[1] Anderson, Douglas D. "A Stone Age Campsite at the Gateway to America" *Scientific American*, V. 218, #6, June 1968, pp. 24-33

*Caribou skins drying
Barrow
March 1974*

90 DISH
Spruce wood painted red and black.
6⅜" (16.3 cm.) long
c. 1935
Kuskokwim River
Newark Museum; 38.51

A black crow is painted inside the bowl; the black dots are goose eggs stored by the crow. The lines pointing inward towards the crow represent spears. The reverse side of the bowl has a face on the bottom and alternating red and black triangles on the sides. It is said to tell the story of a man who disappeared when rocks fell on a cave he entered. The man and the crow mated and their offspring were the Nelson Island people.

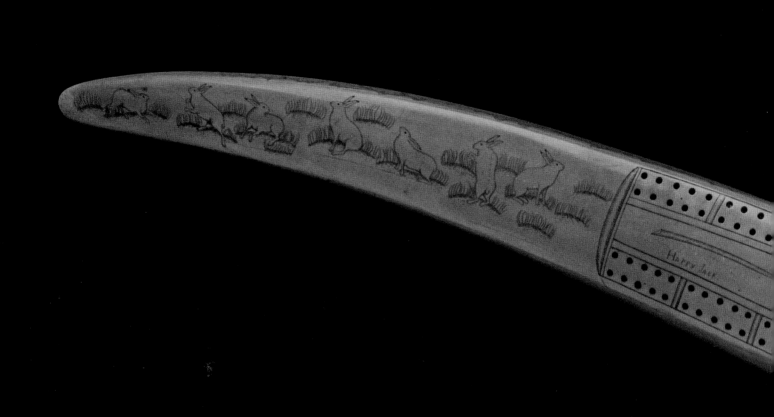

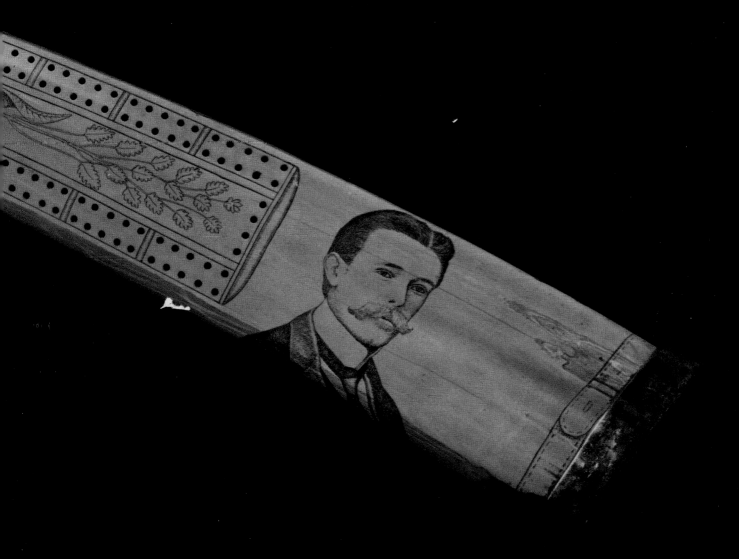

199

199 CRIBBAGE BOARD
Walrus ivory tusk with black engraving
23¼" (59.1 cm.) long
Signed "Happy Jack"
Late 19th or early 20th century
Collection on loan to
The Newark Museum

*"Happy Jack" or Angohwazhuk (c. 1870-
1918), an Eskimo from Little Diomede
Island, is thought to have been the first
Eskimo to carve cribbage boards. He was
influenced by scrimshaw made by American whalemen after he made several
voyages to San Francisco on board a
whaling ship. This cribbage board was
made between 1892-1918. The lifelike
portrait engraved on the right was
undoubtedly copied from an advertise-
ment or a photograph.*

**199a DETAIL OF REVERSE LEFT
SIDE OF CRIBBAGE BOARD
BY "HAPPY JACK"**

*Engraved walruses, beautifully
modelled, basking on the ice.*

**199b DETAIL OF REVERSE RIGHT
SIDE OF CRIBBAGE BOARD
BY "HAPPY JACK"**

*Seals on the ice. The seal at the
extreme right is holding a fish in
his mouth.*

199a

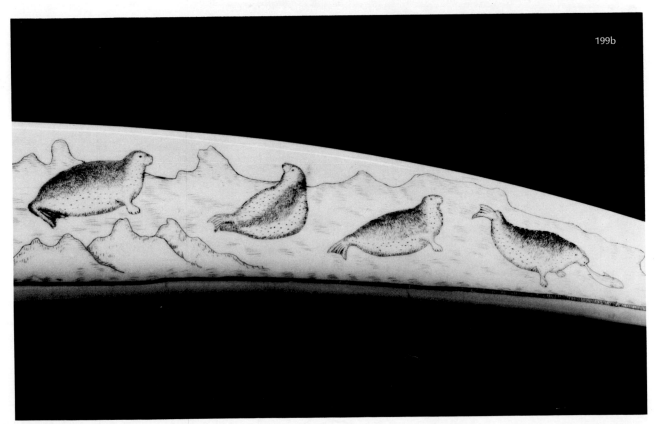

199b

Although mosquito-breeding bogs and pools dot the surface of the marshy tundra in the summer, the ground below remains permanently frozen.

In the past (and to a considerable extent today), the coastal peoples depended largely upon sea mammals for food and fuel, especially the seal, the whale and the walrus. Arctic fish also comprised a large part of their diet, although the Eskimos are primarily meat-eaters. ("Eskimo" is an Indian word meaning "eater of raw meat." The Eskimos call themselves Iñupiat—or Inuit—which means "real people.") In the interior, large herds of caribou, together with the Arctic fox, the rabbit, the wolverine, the squirrel and other small mammals, provided not only meat but the warmest furs from which clothing was traditionally fashioned. Thousands of birds that summered in Alaska were a source of additional food and skins. In former years, if sufficient food were not taken during the warmer, daylight months and preserved or stored for use in the winter months, starvation often ensued.

In contrast to the extreme north of Alaska, the southern Eskimos live in a more hospitable clime. Although temperatures are still very cold in winter, there are many more hours of daylight, trees flourish, salmon and other fish abound in rivers and seas, and land and sea mammal life is plentiful. Survival was less risky, probably accounting for the large population and more complex social structure of the southern Eskimo.

Shelter and clothing were extraordinarily well-suited to the climate. Permanent winter dwellings varied in style and material according to their location and the availability of natural resources, but were usually built of sod, skins, driftwood, whale bones or stone, and were often half-buried underground for warmth and protection from storms. They were lit and well-heated by seal oil or wood burned in small lamps. In summer, people moved to camps or lived in tents, enjoying the outdoors as they led a semi-nomadic life in search of food. Alaskan Eskimos have never lived in igloos, or snow houses, except to seek temporary shelter.

Eskimo society was structured around the family, consisting of parents, children, grandparents, siblings, cousins and other blood and marriage relations, with whom they lived in close proximity. Although divorce and adoption were frequent, all kinship relations, once established, remained in force until death. Cooperative interdependence among members of a family group was essential for survival, but wars and feuds were common among non-related peoples.

There were no chiefs as such. Those men most proficient as hunters and those who were able to exercise intelligence and the best judgment in the activities of life became leaders by virtue of their abilities.

Many of the Eskimos' spiritual beliefs were shaped by their need to obtain food. Reflecting their preoccupation with the animals they depended upon for survival, the Eskimos developed a highly ritualistic but individualized relationship with the spirit forces they associated with the animals. Charms and fetishes were used as intermediaries in order to facilitate their capture and to appease their spirits. The animals were supposed capable of assuming human form. Many men also believed themselves to have an animal self, revealed to them through visions, into which they could turn at will. Shamans (*angatkut*) were thought to have mystical powers giving them supernatural control over physical forces and events.

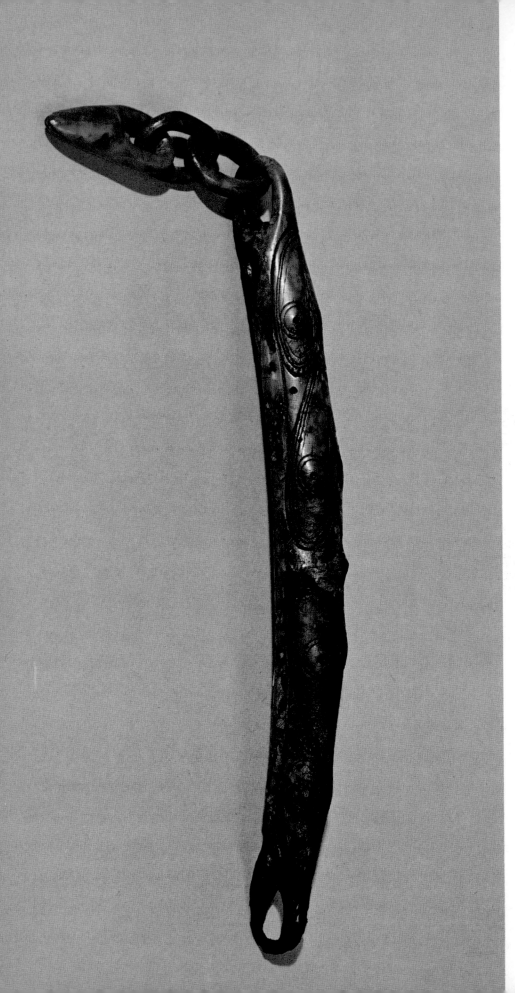

85 BUCKET HANDLE AND CHAIN
Walrus ivory
Handle: 7⅞" (20.02 cm.) long
Chain: 3⅜" (8.58 cm.)
Old Bering Sea (c. 500 A.D.)
Collected at Miyowagh, St. Lawrence
Island, 1950's
Anonymous loan

*One of the most beautiful examples
of Old Bering Sea style, characterized
by graceful curving lines and circles
surrounding raised prominences in an
overall symmetrical design.*

123 DOLL'S PARKA
Tailored coat of matched black
throated loon skins with beaver
fur trim, blue wool yarn ties.
11½" (29.3 cm.) long
c. 1935
Kuskokwim River
Newark Museum; 38.67

*Exquisite workmanship was lav-
ished on this article of doll's
clothing. European influence is
evident in the open front design
of the garment.*

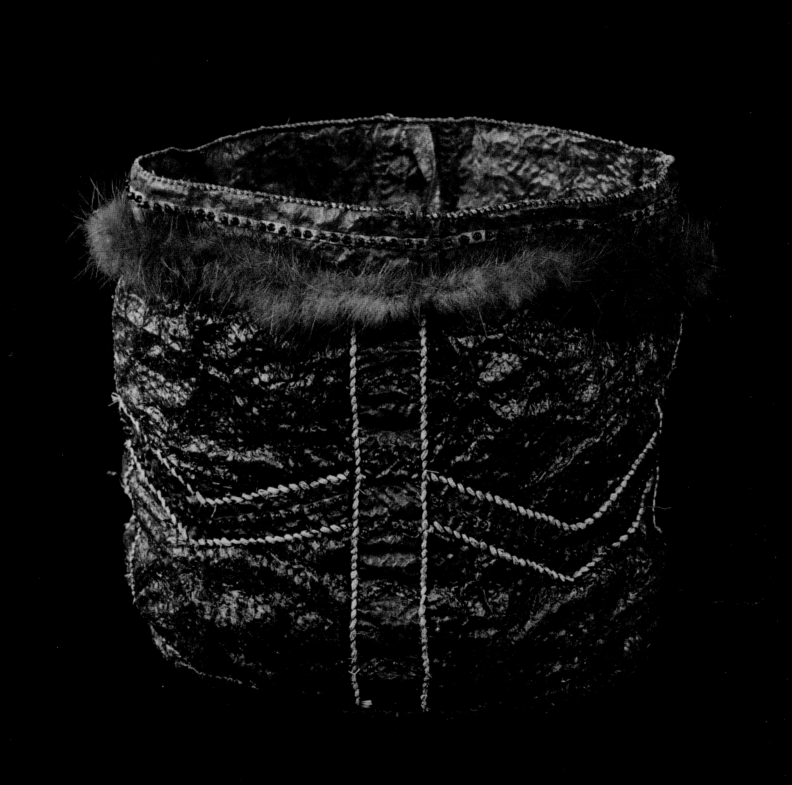

From prehistoric times, men fashioned tools and weapons from the natural materials available to them. The very earliest of the Eskimo implements uncovered in archaeological excavations are similar to some found in Siberia and are purely functional and undecorated. Dating from about 300 B.C., however, objects of amazing beauty have been discovered on both St. Lawrence Island and the Alaskan mainland. They are carved for the most part of walrus ivory, which has turned a dark, rich brown over the centuries, or sometimes of bone or antler. Many of these superbly crafted and ornamented artifacts are also clearly functional in nature, but the use of other objects is unknown to us. As well, beginning from the same period, there exist figurines of people and animals which probably were intended to be religious or ceremonial fetishes.

Ancient Eskimo artifacts frequently were engraved with designs or shapes that have unique stylistic characteristics according to the culture which produced them. Configurations of lines and motifs recur sufficiently that dating of an object often can be based upon its artistic style.

The Eskimo has an extraordinarily keen visual perception of the world around him. This is essential to survival in the arctic desert, and it also enabled him to reproduce in the difficult media faithful representations of what he saw and experienced in his daily existence or in his imagination.

Today considered as "art" because of their great beauty and fine craftsmanship, these objects were not made for art's sake in the Western sense of creating something whose beauty alone is sufficient reason for its being. Their quality arose mainly from the early Eskimo's need to do his utmost to please and satisfy unseen powers in order to guarantee his survival, and from his own innate sensitivities. Artistic inspiration, coming from some deep well-spring of aesthetic ideal in all peoples and which appears basic to man's nature, was notably nurtured by the Eskimos.

Eskimo artistic expression was not limited to carving or handcraft. Because he had no written language (today the Eskimo languages in Alaska are written phonetically in the Roman alphabet), the history and the cultural heritage of his people were passed on through story-telling, dance and song, each raised to a highly developed art form. As well as providing pleasure, Eskimo dancing was another aspect of religious ceremony, creating a further bond between the human and spiritual worlds.

The Eskimo, despite his rigorous existence, has always been a highly gregarious and fun-loving individual. Jokes, games and sports—for enjoyment as well as to develop skills, strength and endurance essential for survival—were extremely popular throughout the Arctic and continue to be so. And delightful toys for children's play, often a reproduction in miniature of the grown-up world, have been made since early prehistoric times.

Many of these traditional patterns of Eskimo life have disappeared over time to be replaced by white man's culture and values. But certain of the old ways have endured, and some aspects of life today have continued in much the same paths as formerly.

Survival of a Culture

Long before white people first discovered Alaska, successful Eskimo adaptation to the environment had already resulted in the development of a rich and unique culture. It could have been expected that without outside influence, as long as the environment in which they lived remained essentially unchanged, a slow process of continual modification of this culture would have proceeded but basically the Eskimo's life would have continued in most respects similar to the past.

Such, however, was not to be. As late as the beginning of the 19th century, when Russian and European explorers and fur trappers first began coming to Alaska in numbers, Eskimo life was much as it must have been in prehistoric times. But contact with the early whites almost immediately modified indigenous life by introducing new material goods as items of trade. The Eskimos were quick to adopt firearms and improved metal tools, recognizing their superiority over traditional implements. At the same time, tobacco, alcohol and white diseases infiltrated Eskimo society. The impact of a foreign culture, however, did not become extremely marked until the second half of the 19th century when white whalers penetrated Western Arctic coastal waters and the contiguous land.

By the mid-1800's, commercial whaling had so greatly exploited the traditional whaling grounds around the globe that it had become increasingly difficult to fill ships' holds with the precious oil and whalebone, or baleen. The opening of the Arctic Ocean to whaling in 1848 brought an ever-increasing number of American whaling ships in search of the Bowhead Whale, a hitherto untapped resource. The Bowhead is a large, relatively slow-swimming whale yielding great amounts of oil and baleen. It summers in the Arctic Ocean after migrating northward through the Bering Strait in the spring, and returns south in the fall. During the two or three months when these waters are largely clear of ice and navigable, the whalers came in numbers. Eventually, they even established shore stations on the Alaskan coast and employed the Eskimos in their enterprise.

These white men effected great changes in almost all aspects of Eskimo life. They whaled so assiduously and so well that in a comparatively brief period of time the Bowhead was almost eliminated from Arctic waters. The whalers then began to hunt the walrus in search of oil, thus further endangering the Eskimos' food supply. They introduced many hitherto unknown diseases to the Native population which had no resistance to the unfamiliar maladies, and large numbers of people died. And they spread the use of whisky among the Eskimos, a destructive influence upon their lives into present times.

On the other hand, the Eskimos, who had hunted the whale and the walrus for a thousand years or more with nothing but ivory or stone-tipped harpoons and spears, learned the use of the darting gun (a hand-thrown metal, toggle-headed harpoon, with a bomb attached that is triggered to explode a few seconds after impact), firearms and the more efficent metal cutting spades and knives. These weapons considerably increased their chances for success in the hunt.

It is noteworthy that whaling continues today as the most important hunting activity and aspect of subsistence living among the Eskimos of northwest Alaska, and that it is carried out in much the same manner as 100 years ago. The Eskimos from the regions of Point Hope, Barrow and St. Lawrence Island have traditionally been whalers. From about mid-April to the end of May the efforts of every able-bodied man and boy are directed towards catching the Bowhead and the smaller Beluga, or white whale. When open lanes

147 FINGER MASK
Wood painted blue with red triangles outlined in pencil; tufts of reindeer beard hair and arctic owl feathers.
4½" (11.5 cm.) height of wood
c. 1935
Kuskokwim River
Newark Museum; 38.348 a,b

These delicate fan-like masks were worn on their fingers by women in dances in which only their arms and upper bodies moved.

of water, called leads, appear close to the shore in the spring, each whaling captain *(umialik)* makes ready his equipment and assembles his crew. The crew usually consists of six to eight men (members of the umialik's family when possible) for whose maintenance he is responsible during the whaling season. The umialik must be a good hunter and also a rich man, for whaling equipment is expensive to purchase and maintain. The umialik has thus traditionally been a leader in his community.

On the mainland, the men establish camp alongside a lead on the sea ice from which they hunt, sometimes several miles from the village; on St. Lawrence Island the leads appear right along shore. The whales are pursued from a skin-covered boat *(umiak)* which is constructed of a wooden frame between 20-30 feet long (formerly driftwood but now largely processed lumber) covered with seal skins or female walrus skins. It is propelled with oars and sail, although an outboard motor is now used to pull a dead whale along shore.

The old men stay on shore with binoculars watching for whales and the movements of the treacherous sea ice; on St. Lawrence Island they communicate with the skin boats through new walkie-talkies.

The whales are sometimes more than twice as long as the boat and the men still hunt them with the antique darting guns or shoulder guns, but they are intrepid in their pursuit. The whale when killed is cut up on the shore or on the sea ice. It is then divided among the crew that killed it and the other assisting crews according to pre-determined shares. On St. Lawrence Island, each whale caught by either of the two main villages on the island is shared with the other village. In Point Hope and Barrow, large whaling festivals are held at the end of the season where meat and *muktuk* (an Eskimo delicacy consisting of whale skin with about an inch of blubber attached) from the year's catch are shared with all visitors. Thus, ancient systems of cooperation and sharing are prolonged into the modern day and generosity is still a quality of the successful hunter.

Whaling means many things to an Eskimo. Whales are an important source of meat and muktuk; they also provide blubber for oil, and baleen from which items for sale are made. Whaling is a link to the past and the ancient culture. And whaling is a way for a man to have pride in himself, to know who he is as a man and an Eskimo.

However, the impact of whaling upon the existing whale population has become a matter of grave concern among scientists and governments. The issue is of great importance to the Eskimo. Research is proceeding both privately and by the U.S. Government to estimate the initial Bowhead population in the Western Arctic through historical records and also to determine insofar as possible the present stock size. Despite the lack of precise figures, it is generally agreed that the current stock is greatly reduced from what it was when commercial Arctic whaling began in the mid-19th century.

In the United States, the Marine Mammal Protection Act of 1972 and the Endangered Species Act of 1973 prohibit commercial whaling of the Bowhead but allow Native peoples living in coastal areas to hunt for subsistence or for the purpose of using whale products to create authentic articles of art and handcraft.

Preliminary research indicates that Alaskan Eskimos now take an average of approximately 30-40 Bowheads annually. There is some indication that the annual catch may be increasing since greater opportunities to obtain paying jobs have made it possible for more men to build and equip boats for the hunt. But there is significant disagreement among researchers as to how many more whales are struck and lost for each animal taken, various estimates of loss rate placing the ratio at anywhere from 1 to 4 lost for each whale recovered.

If, in course, concern over the Bowhead population points toward stricter governmental regulation of whale hunting, the Natives themselves will obviously have a strong interest, along with biologists and ecologists, in what management decisions ought to be taken. Concern over environment is one of the more positive aspects of contemporary life. But the Eskimo, in his tradition and through his culture, is an integral part of his environment, and conservation of the whale has also to be compatible with the preservation of this aspect of Eskimo life.

From 1867, when the United States purchased Alaska from Russia and it became an American Territory, white missionaries and teachers came in increasing numbers to introduce the Christian religion, the English language, and Western goals of education in a well-meaning attempt to suppress and replace the old beliefs in order to prepare the Eskimos for life in "modern" times. Children once learned by observing their elders—the boys to hunt, fish and carve; the girls mainly to sew skins and prepare food. But children who go to school have little time to learn the skills necessary for subsistence survival and difficulty arose in communication and understanding between the older and younger generations. Too, children were forcibly separated from their families if they wished to pursue their education beyond the elementary grades in order to attend high schools which were located in only a few towns in the vast area of Alaska.

The pride of the Eskimo in being part of the natural order of the world was giving way to feelings of inadequacy when confronted with the new standards being taught in church and school.

In addition, the Eskimo learned the use of and became increasingly dependent upon material goods which he no longer feels he can do without. The old-style houses have been replaced by above-ground, contemporary wooden structures which no longer can be heated adequately by a seal oil lamp, so he must have fuel for warmth. He must have a gun and bullets with which to hunt. He must have tea, coffee, sugar and flour with which to supplement his native foods. He must have gasoline with which to run the snowmobile he now uses for transportation instead of the dog team and sled. He keeps in communication with the events of the outside world through radios. He often wears store-bought clothing, not only because it looks more American, but because many of the women no longer sew skins and many of their men no longer hunt to supply them with the skins to sew.

Besides these material changes, contact with the white men in the 19th century caused a revolution in the Eskimo's art. Hitherto, beautiful objects were made for the Eskimo himself to use in his daily life or to serve his religious needs. But outsiders saw the value of an intricately carved or engraved piece of ivory or of a beautifully sewn skin garment and were willing to buy them or trade white man's tools and goods for them. The Eskimo, adaptable and skilled, seized the opportunity to obtain the items which would make his life easier or pleasanter and began to fashion objects that were no longer what he himself needed for his physical or spiritual well-being, but were made

Umiak *with raised sail hunting
for whales. Off Gambell,
St. Lawrence Island
April 1975*

134   BELT FASTENER
Walrus ivory
2⅜" (6.04 cm.) long
Old Bering Sea (c. 500 A.D.)
Collected at Miyowagh, St. Lawrence
Island, 1950's
Anonymous loan
*An exquisitely delicate and beautiful
example of form and Old Bering Sea
design. The fluted edges are most
unusual.*

for sale. Reflecting his dexterity and his personal standards of excellence, many of these 19th century pieces were exquisitely crafted and are considered among the finest examples of Eskimo art. But where the Eskimo continued to express his inner needs in terms of his traditional society, that is, in the creation of masks for religious and ceremonial purposes, he surpassed himself in vigorous, imaginative representation of his spiritual beliefs, and the surviving masks of the 19th and early 20th centuries are among the most powerful examples of Eskimo creativity.

As well, the Eskimo was influenced by the whaleman's scrimshaw carvings and engravings, and a different style of artistic expression came into being around the turn of the 20th century. Although some carvings had been highly realistic since ancient times, Eskimo graphic engraving on ivory in the middle of the 19th century had been characterized by semi-stylized depictions of human beings, animals and their surroundings, usually engraved upon ivory drill bows or pipes (which were not meant to be smoked). Now a pictorial style similar to naturalistic Western drawing emerged where figures were modelled and lifelike, and sometimes were based on actual photographs. Art was signed for the first time. And new forms foreign to the Eskimo, such as cribbage boards, made their appearance. According to Dorothy Jean Ray[2], the first cribbage boards may have been carved around 1900 by Happy Jack *(Angokwazhuk)*, an Eskimo from Little Diomede Island, after he made several voyages to San Francisco on board a whaling ship. He then taught this style of ivory carving and engraving to others in Nome, creating a new tradition of Eskimo art which has affected ivory carving to the present day.

Many older men (and some younger ones too) are still carving ivory objects for sale in much the same techniques and for the same reasons as their 19th century forefathers. These carvers often repeat the same items over and over, becoming specialists in depicting perhaps a whale, a bird, a kayak, because they know these pieces sell successfully. It is true that there is little innovation or imagination visible in the constant repetition of the same theme, and that "knickknacks" done without skill or thought constitute much of this "tourist" art. Nevertheless, certain of the better artists and craftsmen (among them Peter Mayac, Aloysius Pikonganna, Lincoln Milligrock, Bernard Katexac and many others) have such high standards of execution that the results are as fine as any Eskimo carving over the years. These artists in the traditional vein are still carving the same subjects as their ancestors did—the animals around them or the activities of Eskimo life—although they are no longer imbued with magical or religious connotations. That Eskimo art is fashioned for sale ought not in itself denigrate its artistic worth any more than the sale of any other art. Considering the change in Native subsistence patterns, these men have chosen either to supplement their living or to support themselves entirely from the proceeds of their art.

This is also true for a small group of men who have learned to combine successfully the Western techniques of drawing and painting with the representation of traditional Eskimo themes. James (Kivetoruk) Moses and his brother-in-law, George Ahgupuk, are among the best-known. Both were brought up according to the old Eskimo ways in a small village, both are crippled from accident and illness, and both use the media of

(2)   Ray, Dorothy Jean. *Artists of the Tundra and the Sea.* Seattle, Washington, University of Washington Press, 1961, pp. 3-12

paint and watercolor to show us delightful pictorial descriptions of former Eskimo life, events and legends.

Despite the upheavals wrought in the 19th century by the superimposition of new ideas and materialism upon a traditional subsistence economy, many of the old values survive and have come even more to the fore in recent years. A man's worth is still judged in part on his prowess as a hunter. Especially in the more remote villages, families remain close-knit; grandparents, parents and children share their lives together. Eskimo children are treated lovingly yet little evidence of "spoiling" appears. The old legends are still told; dance and song as a means of communication have not been lost, and it is touching to see a child dressed in blue jeans shyly sing and dance following the traditional movements of his people. More and more, enlightened teachers have come to realize the value of a child's participation in traditional activities as part of his education. The Eskimos also appreciate how quickly their ancient heritage may be slipping away, and are establishing village high schools and sponsoring university programs to teach Native culture and language to their own people.

The Native population is much larger today than it was at the turn of the century (there are approximately 35,000 Eskimos living in Alaska at present) and is increasing all the time. Although many Eskimos have moved to the larger urban centers of Alaska— Anchorage and Fairbanks—the villages, too, are growing rapidly. This reflects not only advances in health care and a less perilous life, but also the fact that many Eskimos do not want to leave their traditional homes.

In the past ten years, however, concurrent with this reemergence of Native traditional culture, other events of a momentous nature have taken place, with potential to accelerate tremendously the pace of cultural change.

Present Threat to Survival

Since the Statehood Act in 1959 making Alaska the 49th State, the most important effects upon Alaska as a whole—and especially upon its Native population—have been caused by the large-scale discovery of oil and the Alaska Native Claims Settlement Act. The years from 1968 to 1973 were a hectic period of transition away from continuity with the past and towards an uncertain future.

In 1968, a discovery oil well at Prudhoe Bay on the North Slope of the Brooks Range close to the Arctic Ocean proved up a 10-billion barrel oil field, the largest in North America.[3] The Prudhoe Bay field is expected to produce upwards of 1½ million barrels of crude oil daily. But before the first barrel of oil could be produced, a pipeline had to be constructed to link the producing field in the north with an ice-free port in the south. Construction of the 800 mile, $7.7 billion pipeline—across tundra, rugged mountains, and rivers that were icebound in winter and roaring torrents in spring—was to test severely the technical and engineering capabilities of the oil industry.

The pipeline posed many threats to the environment. Pipe could be buried in solidly frozen ground (permafrost), but the flow of hot oil through the line would melt

[3]   Total United States oil reserves at the time were slightly over 30 billion barrels.

141   HUMAN HEAD
Walrus ivory with incised lines
2½" (6.5 cm.) high
Old Bering Sea (c. 500 A.D.)
St. Lawrence Island
University of Alaska Museum,
Fairbanks; 1-1931-961

Tattoo marks, such as those incised on this magnificent miniature head, were common until recent years. Older women on St. Lawrence Island can still be seen with their chins, cheeks and hands tattooed.

the permafrost, perhaps unevenly, depending on ice content. Elevated, the pipe might prove a barrier to migrating caribou. Crossing rivers, a pipeline leak could pollute waters and despoil fish upon which many villages were dependent.

The harsh environment was seen to be a fragile environment. Selection of pipeline route and determination of engineering specifications threatened to be a long, drawn-out process, hampered by resistance from both ecologists and Natives.

The oil industry, heavily committed financially, was obviously concerned to get production going. The State of Alaska was no less impatient to get its oil royalties and tax revenues. The U.S. Government was also interested in North Slope production in order to reduce national dependence on imported oil from insecure foreign sources of supply. Eventually, Congress was to resolve the issue by legislation that by-passed the many administrative and judicial bottlenecks that might otherwise have prolonged the uncertainty. The Trans-Alaska Pipeline Act was signed in November 1973.

As a result, thousands of new residents and millions of new dollars entered the State. The cost of living skyrocketed for whites and Natives alike in what had already been the most expensive region of the United States. At the same time, many high-paying jobs became available for enterprising and capable Natives, providing a new source of sorely-needed cash for their families. For the men who work, however, pipeline and related jobs cause them to be away from home for long periods of time, thus weakening family structure. And, if they decide to go back to their villages for hunting or whaling at certain seasons of the year, as many would like to do, they are considered unreliable and irresponsible by white standards. The large influx of transient population has also had the unpleasant effect of introducing drugs to the Alaskan Natives, and it is a shocking reminder of urban 20th century life to realize that a "drug problem" exists among some of the youth in tiny and remote Eskimo villages.

It was also in the late 1960's and early 1970's that Alaskan Native land claims came to a head, and not by mere coincidence. For hundreds of years, the Natives of Alaska had lived on the land and from the land, but with no formal or legal entitlement to the land of which they were an integral part. The 1867 Treaty of Cession, by which the United States acquired Alaska from Russia, provided that inhabitants who remained in the ceded territory should be admitted to all the rights, advantages and immunities of citizens of the United States—with the exception of "uncivilized native tribes."[4]

It was not until the Organic Act of 1884, wherein Congress replaced military by civilian government in Alaska, that the first recognition was accorded to Native land rights:

> "Indians or other persons in said district shall not be disturbed in the possession of any lands actually in their use or occupation or now claimed by them, but the terms under which such persons may acquire title to such lands is reserved for future legislation by Congress."[5]

Another 85 years were to pass before such "future legislation" was enacted. The

[4] Hensley, William L. (Igagruk), "What Rights to Land Have the Alaskan Natives?" (May 1966). In *Alaska Native Land Claims. Hearings before the Committee on Interior and Insular Affairs U.S. Senate, 90th Congress, 2nd Session on S. 2906.* February 8, 9, 10, 1968. Washington, D.C., Government Printing Office, 1968, pp. 66-74.

[5] Act of May 17, 1884, Sec. 8, 23 Stat. 26. Quoted in *Ibid*, p. 68.

Alaska Native Claims Settlement Act was passed in December 1971 in the heat of controversy over the oil pipeline. Alaskan Natives—Eskimos, Indians and Aleuts—were given first right of selection over 40 million acres of Federal land (the State's selection of Federal lands as provided in the Statehood Act was to come after the Native selection) and were further awarded close to $1 billion in cash. The money was intended to be about equally divided between outright Federal cash grants over an 11-year period and a 2% entitlement to revenues from subsequent leasing and development of government lands.

The instruments through which the settlement was to be effected were the Native Regional Corporations. Twelve were organized, roughly paralleling established Native settlements and groups. The Native Regional Corporation was to be a profit-making entity by law, charged with responsibility for selecting the land and managing the money granted by the Act. Stockholders were to be Native men, women and children in each region who enrolled by a certain date.[6] Thus, the largest private engineering project in history, the oil pipeline, was paralleled by the creation of Native Corporations similarly dedicated to the profitable investment of their assets in commercial undertakings.

But what does all this have to do with the Eskimo way of life? No Eskimo had ever before exercised restrictive "ownership" over his ancestral land or thought of exploiting its resources. He led a semi-nomadic existence, going where he pleased, hunting and fishing for his subsistence according to what the land would provide. And although the Eskimo has long enjoyed accumulating wealth and property, he was certainly not oriented towards choosing the highest-yielding, profit-making investments or to the world of high finance.

These are abrupt and dramatic changes from all that had gone before. Profits realized by the Native Corporations from the development of petroleum or mineral reserves eventually could be applied to health, educational and social projects of enormous benefit to their own population. But if Native culture is going to survive in any way similar to the past, the people's identification with the land, and their right to continue their traditional patterns of hunting and fishing, will have to be protected. Judicious management of the land and natural resources is evidently of primary importance. To insure their participation in decisions involving the safeguarding of their ancient heritage, new militants have arisen among Native groups. The question is asked urgently, "Does One Way of Life Have to Die so Another Can Live?"[7]

The status in 1976 of Alaskan Native arts and handcrafts reflects the changing quality of Eskimo life and the dichotomy as well as the continuity between old and new. Traditional ivory carvers and engravers still practice their ancient crafts. Conscious and serious attempts are being made to revive the old techniques of basket-making, skin-sewing, pottery-making, as well as to teach carving and printmaking, through workshops and courses in both urban and rural Alaska. Several formalized art training programs exist. Periodic art festivals and conferences are held with exhibits and demonstrations,

(6)   There are presently 13 regional corporations, the 13th consisting of those persons who are at least one quarter Native, but who either live outside the State and/or who choose not to be affiliated with any particular region.

(7)   Yupiktak Bista. *Does One Way of Life Have to Die so Another Can Live?* A report on subsistence and the conservation of the Yupik life-style. Bethel, Alaska, 1975.

and the juried Annual Alaska Native Arts and Crafts Festival held at the Anchorage Museum of Historical and Fine Arts provides an outlet for the finest items.

In addition to the traditionally-oriented artists and craftsmen, who are largely self-taught, there are a number of young Native artists working in a more modern idiom. Most of these men have studied in art schools and universities in Alaska and the Lower 48 States, and have been exposed to the theories and the history of Western art.

Ronald Senungetuk, an Eskimo formerly from the village of Wales, Alaska, who is both a teacher and an accomplished artist, has given voice to a sentiment that exists among some of this contemporary group to the effect that they are not "Eskimo artists" but artists who are also Eskimos. This is not just a matter of semantics, for it means that they wish to be free to express themselves as artists whether or not that expression coincides with what hitherto has been thought of as "Eskimo art." Mr. Senungetuk himself, trained in the United States and Norway, produces beautiful works of art in silver or in wood which do not look "Eskimo" at all.

Other fine young artists, all represented in major Alaskan museum collections although perhaps not as yet too well-known outside the State—Larry Ahvakana, Melvin Olanna, Joseph Senungetuk, Sylvester Ayek among others—are working in many non-traditional media and forms but are more apt to return to their Eskimo heritage for subject matter, while presenting it in a new way. These men are distant from their ancestors' conception of art as an intermediary with a spirit world and they have also separated themselves from the pragmatically-inspired 19th century idea of producing art because others want to buy it. They are trying to create what they feel, with inspiration coming from internal sources rather than external considerations. In many cases, this involves a reaffirmation of their Eskimo roots as representing the deepest part of their natures, but it also reflects a Westernized conception of art.

Among the formalized art education programs that exist within Alaska, most important and influential is the University of Alaska's Extension Center in Arts and Crafts at Fairbanks directed by Ronald Senungetuk. The Extension Center provides training in art to students who are not enrolled in an academic course of study. Although it is not limited to Native participants, many of the most active and successful Native artists have been educated there in carving and sculpture, fine printmaking, jewelry design and woodworking. Scholarships have been available for their support.

The University also sponsors the Village Art Upgrade Program which offers limited courses in various arts and crafts, given in the villages themselves, as part of an outreach program of the State Department of Education.

Also noteworthy is the Visual Arts Center of Alaska located in Anchorage, a non-profit corporation and art center (with perpetual funding problems) dedicated to the development of excellent quality creative design and art. The Center provides informal instruction, studios, materials and tools, as well as a small exhibition gallery, and an atmosphere where a free interchange of ideas can flow between the artists working there. Although participants have been largely Native, the Center is open to all serious and qualified Alaskans. The Indian Arts and Crafts Board of the U.S. Department of the Interior formerly had a field representative working with the Visual Arts Center as artist and administrator. This position, once held by Peter Seeganna of Nome, has not been refilled for lack of funds since Seeganna's death.

The arts in Alaska are important. Many Native artists and cultural leaders feel, however, that extant programs are not sufficient for the perpetuation and encouragement of the Native arts in Alaska. They have called for the establishment of an Institute of Alaskan Native Arts where all the arts would be taught in a framework of Native culture and which would offer a comprehensive accredited educational program according to the Natives' own desires and needs. A preliminary study has been completed[8] which has reported favorably on the advisability and the feasibility of such an Institute. But despite wide-spread enthusiasm for the project, there is also opposition on the grounds that it would even further distinguish and separate the Native or Eskimo artist from the international community of his fellow artists.

Conclusion

It seems evident that the changes now occurring in Alaska are affecting much more than the traditional material culture of the Eskimos. Side by side with the onslaught upon the underlying foundations of their society, however, there is emerging a new reaffirmation of self, not exactly in the old image but no longer content to follow the white man's path. The Eskimo, adaptable through his thousands of years' old history to the demands his environment and life have placed upon him, will undoubtedly emerge from this period of accelerated change an altered but proud representative of a viable people. It is impossible to predict the direction the Eskimo's cultural adaptation will take. His own heritage of survival in the Arctic and his own perception of life will shape his future. If art can be considered as a statement of man's inner self and his culture, then Eskimo art will also adapt itself to the Eskimo's self-image and new way of life. In the long run, the only valid answer to the question, "What does it mean to be an Eskimo?," may be to consider oneself an Eskimo, and that will be definition enough.

BARBARA LIPTON
August 1976

[8]   Institute of Alaskan Native Arts Committee. *Report of the Institute of Alaskan Native Arts Committee on a Study of the Proposed Development of an Educational Institution for: Native Culture in the State of Alaska.* Fairbanks, Alaska, 1975.

CONVERSATION WITH AN ALASKAN NATIVE ARTIST: LAWRENCE AHVAKANA

This conversation was held at the Visual Arts Center, Anchorage, Alaska, between Lawrence Ahvakana and Barbara Lipton on May 21, 1976. It was recorded and edited by Mrs. Lipton and submitted for review to Mr. Ahvakana in June 1976. At the time, Mr. Ahvakana was Sculptor-in-Residence at the Visual Arts Center and was on the Board of Trustees of the Anchorage Fine Arts and Historical Museum.

Question: What do you think is the difference between traditional Eskimo art and art being done by younger Eskimos today?

L.A. Well, you have to realize there's a lot of different cultures involved in the art that's being done now. It is true that the traditional ivory carving is still being done by some of the younger generation and they learn from the older people what it is to carve and that you can make a living on carving alone. I think, though, that there's a few people—like myself—who think of art in a different way, as an aspect of an artist's feelings instead of just using it for monetary gain. For me, it's more of a struggle to try to make something out of stone and to try to understand it than to think about what the price is. I'm trying more to develop what I've been taught in art school and through the different people that I've met. I feel that I'm not separated from the older ideas of the Eskimo culture, though, except for maybe growing up mostly in a different atmosphere. But I don't feel separated from my ancestors and from their culture and I don't feel that I'm doing more or better. I'm just doing something for myself that's different. But still, I am the culture and I'm as part of it as a piece of ivory, even though my work is different. So it's no use trying to separate the feelings of old and young.

Question: Although your art is certainly not the traditional kind of Eskimo carving, in your works you tend to use subject matter relating to your own culture. This must be very important to you.

L.A. Oh, yes. Like, for a lot of people their second person is an animal. I have a second person. I think it's a seal, or an owl. And I use those animals a lot within my sculpture pieces and I try to make it realistic. It's not a fairy tale that I'm going through. It's real, because I've felt it many times and I've felt it while I'm hunting. So I'm trying to understand more of myself, I guess, and just trying to understand what my surroundings are, what influences me, when I work.

Question: Tell me a little about yourself, your family and your background?

L.A. I was born on July 8, 1946. I'm thirty years old. I grew up in Barrow, Alaska, for seven years and first learned to speak the *Iñupiat* language, and through my grandparents I learned to understand the feelings of what my people really were and what my people were really like, and to understand what the feelings were between us.

My great grandfather on my mother's side was a whaler who came here from

192 SCULPTURE "SHAMAN TURNING
        INTO SEAL"
Ivory and sterling silver
6" x 6" (15.2 cm. x 15.2 cm.)
Lawrence Ahvakana (1946-   )
1975
Collection of the Visual Arts Center of
Alaska, Anchorage

*An ivory shaman with two ivory seals
emerging diagonally from his sides is
seated in front of a sterling silver disk.
Many Eskimos believe that they have a
second self in the form of an animal. This
sculpture unites an ancient religious
belief with modern materials and design.*

England. On my mother's Eskimo side, my great grandfather and great grandmother were *angatkut,* or shamans, medicine men. My mother is Christian but she also believes in the old religions that people tell me are superstitious.

My father is part white also. His mother's father was E. W. Nelson, the archaeologist. My father never carved. He was a pretty good hunter, though, and he taught me how to hunt.

We left Barrow to come to Anchorage where my parents could get a job and get some money and give me a good schooling. I grew up in Anchorage through the grade schools. At first I didn't know how to speak English and I only knew how to speak *Iñupiat,* which is the name of our language, and myself I am *Iñupiak.* The *Iñupiat* are the northern Eskimos from around King Island all the way up north through Canada to Greenland. I graduated from high school in 1966 and from there I went to an art school, the Institute of American Indian Arts in Santa Fe, New Mexico, where I studied sculpture and where I did learn basically all the arts.

I had one instructor I got very close to there, the one who really showed me how to feel and how to understand why I was carving. He taught me that I should put down what I really feel instead of what other people think I should feel. His name is Allan Houser and he's an Apache Indian. I think he's one of the foremost Indian artists and he is one of the first to do his own art according to his own ideas instead of doing a "trinket" art or a used art.

In 1969 I went to Cooper Union in New York City for a year and then I transferred to the Rhode Island School of Design where I studied for two years and got my Bachelor of Fine Arts degree. I was in a group exhibit called *Native North American Art* with some other young Indian artists in the Brooklyn Museum in 1972 and also was in a Smithsonian Portrait Gallery Group show in 1972.

When I graduated from Rhode Island I went back to Barrow. I had a grant from the National Endowment for the Arts to study and work with the people there and to set up a glass blowing workshop. I do traditional glass blowing also, with blow pipes and molten glass. I build furnaces and I can build all the equipment for a glass shop. I built one up in Barrow and for several years I was working with the shop and we did some glass work with the school. I also did some sculpture there. Then I quit and came here to work for the Visual Arts Center and I've been here for a year now. I don't really teach students here. It's more of an artist-to-artist relationship. We teach each other.

Question: You have lived and been educated outside in a white man's world for a long time. How have you been changed by those experiences?

L.A. I don't know. I can't visualize myself in a different place than I've lived. I can't visualize myself living like they did a hundred years ago. But living outside of the culture brings out certain personal feelings more. If I lived up in Barrow I would just kind of take it for granted but when I was living away from it I started getting the feeling of wanting to live in the Eskimo culture. I try to express a lot of feelings for things like Eskimo dancing. I like Eskimo dancing—I get a strong urge to do it hard, and for a long time. Or if something bothers me, then I carve a lot; I get into the stone and I work and work at it to restrengthen myself until I get really tired. I try to do that with my culture also. I try to relate to certain things that are basic in the culture. And from there I can relate to the people better.

Question: Tell me about Eskimo dances. Are they a way of relating history or of telling stories? Are they just for entertainment?

L.A. Dancing is all that. Some people think it's all for relaxation but it isn't. It's a feeling of understanding what your ancestors are telling you. Some of these songs are hundreds of years old and yet they have all the feelings and all the energy of the first day they were made. The younger people especially are understanding more of the language and understanding the older thoughts through the dances. Dancing is one of the oldest cultural forms of our civilization and a lot of the younger people are learning to do our traditional dances from pre-school and grade school all the way up to the elderly people who were told by the missionaries that it was wrong to do them.

Question: Can you discuss any of the special problems of the younger Alaskan Native artists?

L.A. I think one of the problems is not understanding the basic nature of art. The visual arts, working with your hands, haven't really grown much, haven't changed much from carving trinkets, from making other than a seal, other than a bear, other than an ivory piece, other than a basket. I think they should have a good feeling for art, should try to express art in a humanistic way instead of just trying to get the money for it. You can see this partly through an artist's work and partly through himself. That type of feeling hasn't been coming out with the younger people quite as yet.

Question: In order to have a good feeling for, or to understand art, don't you first have to try to understand yourself? Isn't that the problem with some of the younger Native men and women today, that they're not sure exactly who they are?

L.A. Yes, because they haven't been influenced by their own culture. They've been influenced by white culture. They've been influenced by white culture because the white people have the money and the things that the Native people might really need. Or that they'd rather use instead of making something themselves that might take hours to make. Instead of taking care and making something good, they sloppily make something. I can pick out a piece of work that's been sloppily made because I'm a meticulous craftsman. I try to get the best feelings through my craft and the craft is supposed to

JAMES (KIVETORUK) MOSES AND HIS
WIFE, BESSIE
Nome, 1974

*Moses was born in Cape Espenberg
around 1900 and is now living in Nome.
He paints delightful visual depictions of
Eskimo history and legends, sometimes
doing many versions of the same story.
Moses began painting in 1954 after he
was injured in an airplane crash and
could no longer trap animals or fish for
his living.*

206   WATERCOLOR PAINTING "POLAR
      BEAR AND BROWN BEAR FIGHT
      OVER A DEAD WALRUS"
Watercolor and ink on paper
12" x 18" (30.5 cm. x 45.7 cm.) unframed
James (Kivetoruk) Moses (c. 1900-   )
Early 1970's
Collection on loan to
The Newark Museum

*The Eskimo hunter in the background
observed this scene. When he returned
the next day, the two bears had destroyed
each other. Moses has had one-man
exhibitions of his work in the Alaska
State Museum, Juneau, and the Henry Art
Gallery in Seattle.*

28 MALE LOON
Walrus ivory with black engraving,
yellow beak.
3" (7.6 cm.) long
Peter Mayac (c. 1908-   )
1973
Collection on loan to
The Newark Museum

*Peter Mayac is formerly of King Island
and now lives in Anchorage. He is one of
the finest traditional Eskimo carvers and
engravers of ivory and taught at the
University of Alaska's Extension Center
in Arts and Crafts. In poor health, he no
longer is able to do much carving.*

29 EAGLE
Walrus ivory with black engraving, yellow
feet and beak.
3⅛" (7.9 cm.) long
Peter Mayac
1973
Collection on loan to
The Newark Museum

28

29

be perfect. Your personal feelings for the aesthetic nature of the craftsmanship are what count. You feel better when you look at something that's well made, made to touch, where the joints hang together well, where the pieces fit. It would bother me if in the stone you saw little holes or rough file marks, or chips all over it. I take hours and hours just finishing the stone. I might take a month just to finish a stone which, when I sell it, won't give me the amount of money that I worked for. But the feelings I have when I'm doing it is what is important. The outcome is something secondary to the feelings of how you work at it.

Question: What are some of the training programs for today's younger artists? What needs are there for training?

L.A.   The needs are for programs to train children. When you get into the high schools you should have more environmental types of programs like working out of doors or working in a tent somewhere or working with your grandparents.

Question: Well, that is the traditional Eskimo way of learning, isn't it? But do you think there is a need for formal training programs also?

L.A.   Yes, if the individual really wants to get into that, if they want to try to use art as a lifestyle, as a way of making a living and of reacting with yourself and with other people. The University in Fairbanks has programs for that but more strictly on a west-ernized type of art, more visual feelings instead of personal, cultural feeling. That's why a lot of Eskimo villages are getting their own university now. In Barrow, for instance, we have Iñupiat University which is a university for Eskimos and we have an art program and a cultural program run by a young artist who's a dancer and a story teller. Also, they're trying now to build a Native arts school here in Alaska to try to relate the feelings of art with the feelings of our people's culture and not to separate the two. I think it's a good idea.

Question: What do you think is the future for Alaskan Eskimo art?

L.A.   I think it will perpetuate by following whatever social patterns that might develop in the culture and the craft will survive to a certain point and the arts will change and will definitely evolve into something else.

Question: In what way do you see this happening?

L.A.   It's not in a bad way. I never think of it in a bad way. Basically, everything will change. So art will change with it and be stronger towards a certain purpose. I hope it will be more representative of the cultural feelings of our people and that it will help perpetuate the culture. I think that myself, what I'm working at, is my culture. That's what I'm giving to my people. And if they don't understand what I'm doing now and don't enjoy it now, I hope they know that I'm not doing it just to earn a living. I feel good at it.

Question: It is very interesting talking with you. I feel that you have a very deep personal philosophy that's difficult to express. Would you just talk for a while about the things that are important to you?

L.A.   I've just come back from Barrow where I was whaling. I was out there for a whole week with my dad and with some other people in our crew. And then I had to come back to get into some work I was doing here and I only could spend a week up there on the ice and a week in the village. And I had the feeling of why did I have to leave? I was just right in the middle of it there. I had the feeling of being out of place here when I got back and I wanted to be back there in Barrow and work with them. They got a whale when I left and I had the feeling that I should have been there to help cut it up and give it out and to help with the feast. It's hard to understand because the way I've been living here and the way I've been working is completely different and contrary to what's happening back home. So when I'm working on something I try to relate my feelings of what I'm missing. Working with the arts in a way helps me to be with them more. It's like a fetish for me. When I'm working I always think about where I come from and what I'm missing. I start dreaming and I start relating to my work in a different way and then suddenly it starts changing and a piece is coming out good. I'm working on a piece now, a man that's drumming and singing a song because I just started learning how to drum and trying to sing my songs, my mother's songs. My great grandmother made these songs and my mother is the only person that knows them in the family and she wants me to be a part of that and to be a knowledge receiver for the dances and for the songs.

We're not a dying race, we're not a dying people. I think that we can run our own lives. The language is a lot stronger now. Our dance is living and reliving and is being relearned. All these different things come into my mind everyday. I'm just telling you how I feel. As an artist you're supposed to be evaluating and understanding your surroundings.

185   DOUBLE MASK
Wood stained red, black paint,
bird quills, rawhide tie.
12¼" (31.2 cm.) long
c. 1935
Kuskokwim River
Newark Museum; 38.345 a-c

*The combined fish and bird outer
mask has two flippers attached to
the body with bird quills. The back
of the animal is a face which
opens to reveal the face of a
woman stained red. It was
believed that this bird-fish lived in
the ocean. It had no teeth but ate
by sucking flesh from bones.*

187   DOUBLE MASK
Wood painted with black,
rawhide tie.
13" (33 cm.) long
c. 1935
Kuskokwim River
Newark Museum; 38.344 a-c

*The outer mask represents a bird
with spotted tail and head. Two
thumbless hands with a black spot
in the palm project from the body
indicating the belief that game
will be plentiful. The back of the
animal is a face which opens to
reveal an inner mask showing the
face of a man with smiling mouth,
carved teeth and black hair.
Sometimes the shaman's spirit
helper aided him by letting the
doors clap open, thus exposing
the spirit's face.*

185

187

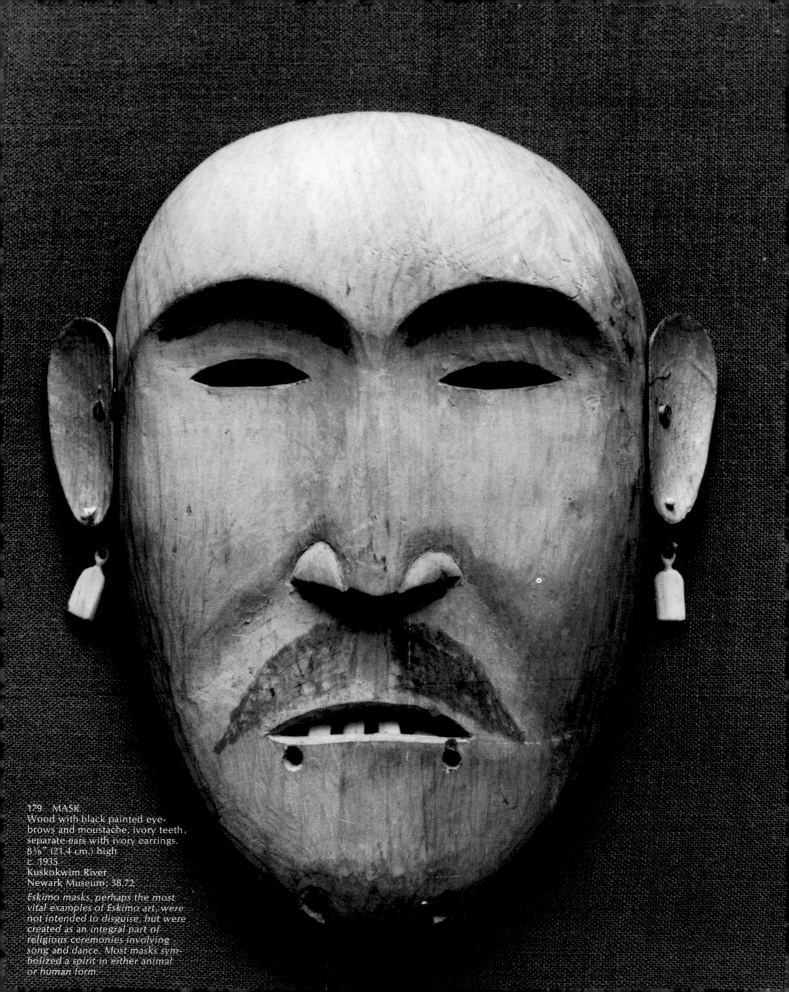

179 MASK
Wood with black painted eye-
brows and moustache, ivory teeth,
separate ears with ivory earrings.
8⅜″ (21.4 cm.) high
c. 1935
Kuskokwim River
Newark Museum; 38.72

*Eskimo masks, perhaps the most
vital examples of Eskimo art, were
not intended to disguise, but were
created as an integral part of
religious ceremonies involving
song and dance. Most masks sym-
bolized a spirit in either animal
or human form.*

102 BAG
Swan's foot skin bag embroidered
with white reindeer hair and red
wool, decorated with white seed
beads around top. Reverse side
has a geometric design with an
overlay of two crossed bird quills.
Two claws are on either side of
bag at top.
6½" (16.6 cm.) high;
7¾" (19.7 cm.) wide
c. 1935
Point Barrow
Newark Museum; 38.66

176 FEMALE FIGURE
Walrus ivory
6¾" (17.2 cm.) high
Okvik (c. 0 A.D.)
Punuk Islands
Collection on loan to
The Newark Museum

*Characteristic of Okvik figurines, this
female has a long, oval face with stylized
features and a straight nose. The body is
unmodeled but parallel incised lines may
represent clothing. She was probably
made as a fetish. The ivory has turned a
dark, rich brown over centuries of burial.*

183 MASK
Wood painted black and red, two
arms and two legs stained red project
from the head.
9¼" (23.2 cm.) high
c. 1935
Kuskokwim River
Newark Museum; 38.346a-e

*The use of parts of the body was
customary to indicate the complete
spirit embodied in the mask.*

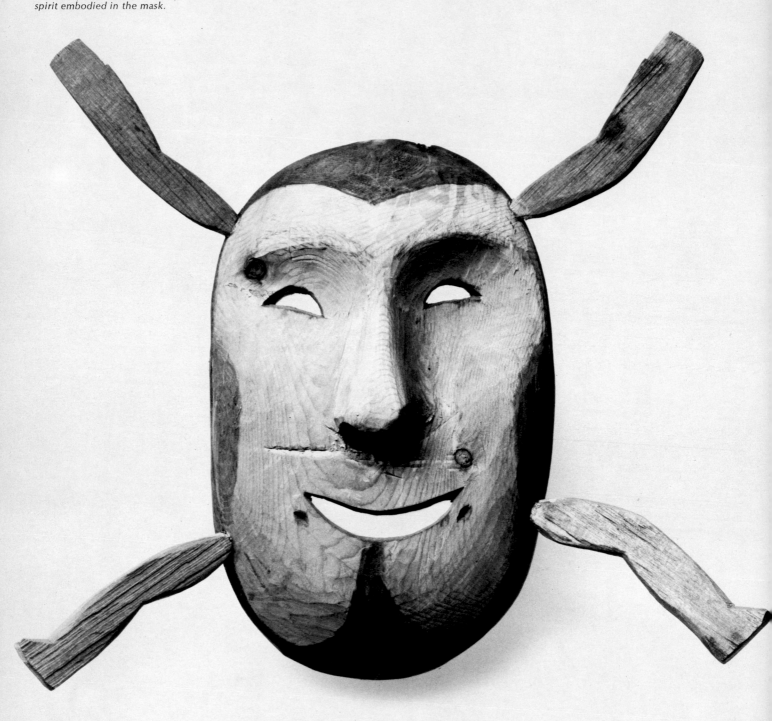

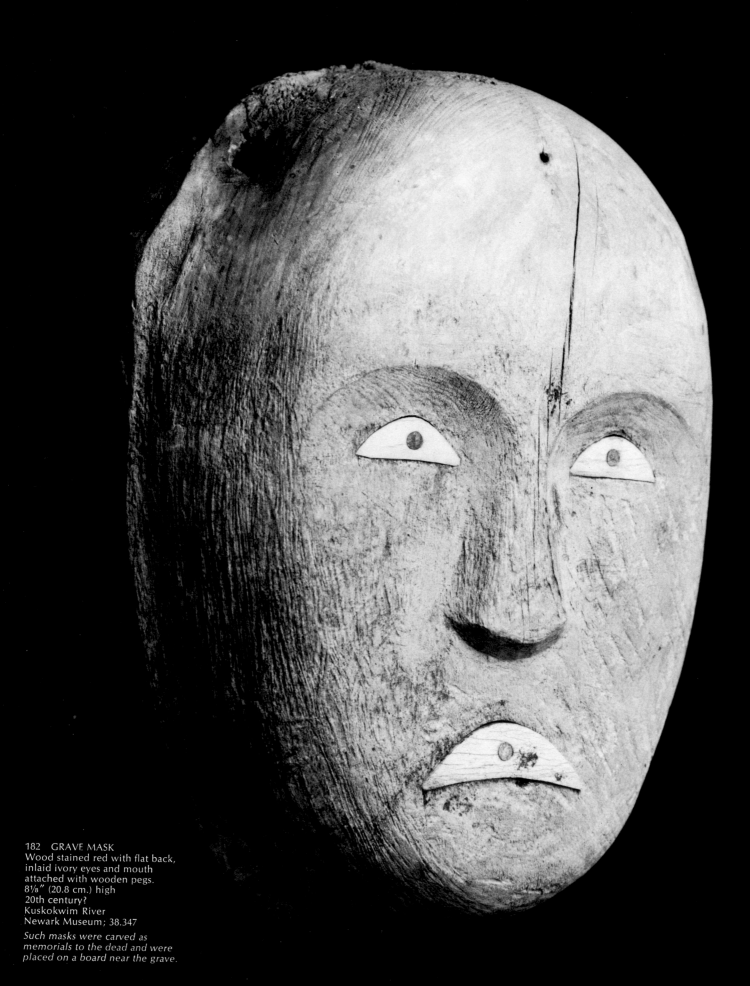

182   GRAVE MASK
Wood stained red with flat back,
inlaid ivory eyes and mouth
attached with wooden pegs.
8⅛" (20.8 cm.) high
20th century?
Kuskokwim River
Newark Museum; 38.347

*Such masks were carved as
memorials to the dead and were
placed on a board near the grave.*

91 DISH
Spruce wood painted red and
black with a land otter painted on
the bottom.
8¾" (22.4 cm.) long
c. 1935
Kuskokwim River
Newark Museum; 38.50

The painting tells the story of an
otter who came back to a lake
hungry. He ate half of each of four
other otters, then ate a nest of
goose eggs in the middle of the
lake. A red band on the reverse of
the bowl is the bloody trail left by
the otter as he circled the lake.

86 SPOON
Wood painted with red and black
design.
10⅛" (25.9 cm.) long
c. 1920
Cape York
Newark Museum; 21.2041

87 SPOON
Musk ox horn spoon with black
engraving around outer edge
showing hunting scenes and
caribou.
8⅝" (22 cm.) long
19th century
Newark Museum: 32.552

This style of 19th century engrav-
ing is similar to that usually found
on ivory pipes or drill bows.

152 LUTE
Wood stained red with black
paint.
17⅝" (44.8 cm.) long
c. 1935
Kuskokwim region
Newark Museum; 38.54

This type of instrument would
have been played by a woman
who fingered and struck the string
with a stick as an accompaniment
to singing. The spruce root string
is missing.

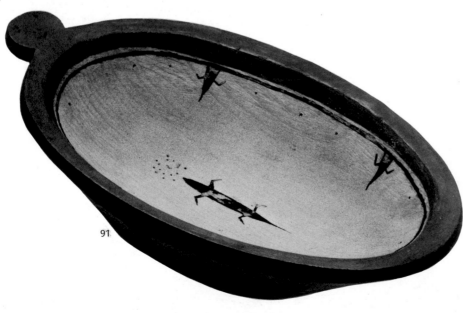

91

86

52

87

152

13

13   SEAL DRAG
Walrus ivory seals with inlaid
baleen eyes and nostrils on a
leather thong.
8½" (21.6 cm.) across
19th century?
Newark Museum; 00.342

*Drag handles were used for
hauling dead seals or other loads
over snow and ice.*

200   CRIBBAGE BOARD
Walrus ivory tusk with carved
figures of a walrus, a fish and a seal
supported on two ivory seals.
Reverse side has black engravings
of walrus, a seal and a polar bear.
Ivory piece inserted at top says
"Nome Alaska 1922"
22⅝" (57.6 cm.) long
1922
Nome
Newark Museum; 23.1387a-h

*Despite the fact that Eskimos carve
many cribbage boards, cribbage is
not an Eskimo game.*

163   STORY KNIFE
Walrus ivory with incised decoration.
13⅜" (34 cm.) long
19th or early 20th century
Kuskokwim River
Newark Museum; 38.338

*Story knives were used by girls to
illustrate stories by drawing
pictures in the snow or mud, and
apparently were found only in
southwestern Alaska.*

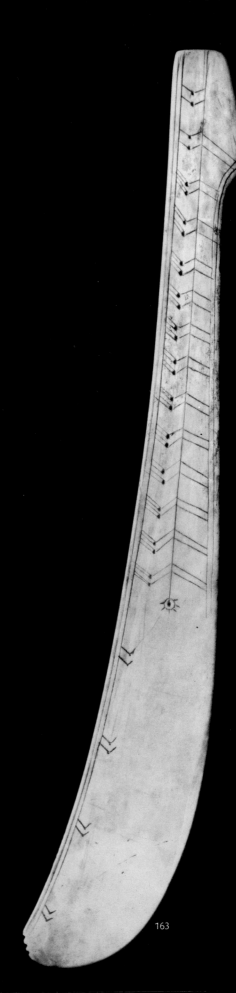

163

178

178 MASK
Wood painted red edged with
reindeer beard hair.
12″ (30.6 cm.) high
c. 1935
Kuskokwim River
Newark Museum; 38.340

180 MASK
Wood stained blue on forehead,
white face. Five appendages
stained blue representing four
flippers and a tail are attached
with bird quills.
12¼″ (31.2 cm.) high
c. 1935
Kuskokwim River
Newark Museum; 38.341 a-f

*This mask represents the "mother
of the mukluk seals" and assured
the shaman that the souls of the
seals were satisfied and that there
would be plenty of meat, oil and
skins. It was used with the
shaman's mask (38.342)*

181 MASK
Wood painted white with red lips
and separate unpainted ears with
string attachments for earrings.
8½″ (21.5 cm.) high
c. 1935
Kuskokwim River
Newark Museum; 38.342

*This mask was worn by a shaman
and was used with the "mother of
the mukluk seals" mask (38.341).*

180

181

148   FINGER MASK
Wood painted red and black;
reindeer beard hair, raven and
arctic owl feathers.
4¾" (12.1 cm.) height of wood
c. 1935
Kuskokwim River
Newark Museum; 38.349 a,b

*Eskimo dancing not only provided
entertainment, but was also an
aspect of religious ceremonialism.
The young people have shown a
renewed interest in recent years
in learning the ancient dances.*

151   DANCE FILLET
Reindeer hair, summer mink, hair
seal, flannel, calico, yarn.
11⅛" (28.3 cm.) wide
c. 1935
Kuskokwim River
Newark Museum; 38.58

*Such fillets were worn on their head
by men during certain ceremonial
dances.*

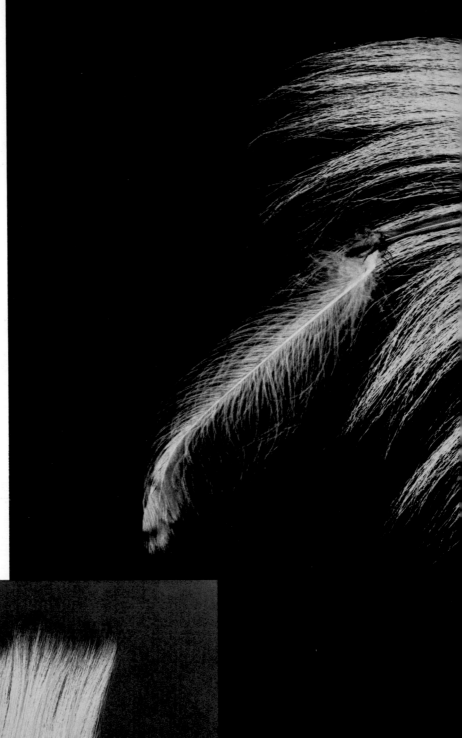

148

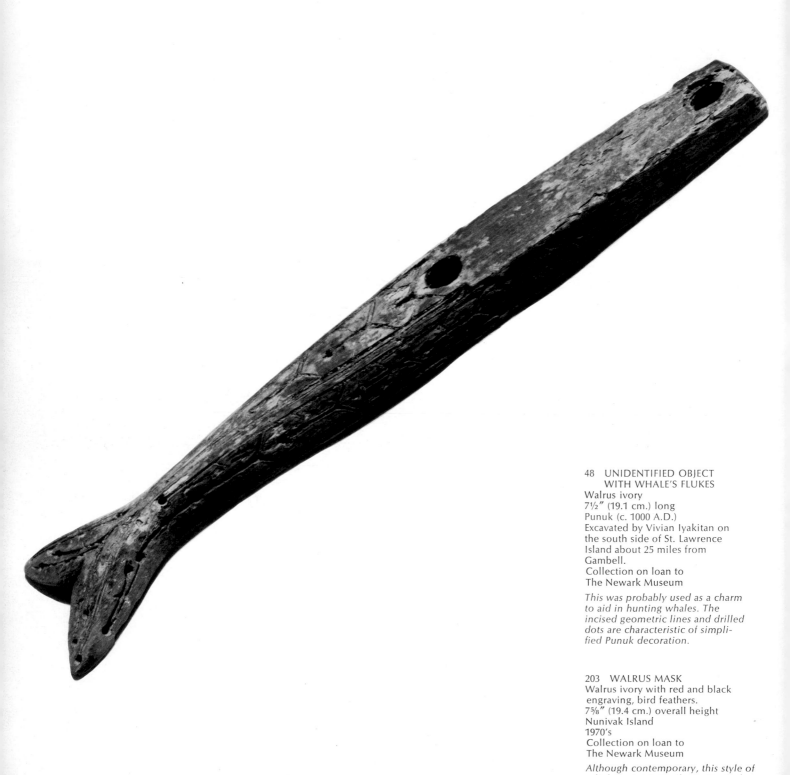

48   UNIDENTIFIED OBJECT
      WITH WHALE'S FLUKES
Walrus ivory
7½" (19.1 cm.) long
Punuk (c. 1000 A.D.)
Excavated by Vivian Iyakitan on
the south side of St. Lawrence
Island about 25 miles from
Gambell.
Collection on loan to
The Newark Museum

*This was probably used as a charm
to aid in hunting whales. The
incised geometric lines and drilled
dots are characteristic of simpli-
fied Punuk decoration.*

203   WALRUS MASK
Walrus ivory with red and black
   engraving, bird feathers.
7⅝" (19.4 cm.) overall height
Nunivak Island
1970's
Collection on loan to
The Newark Museum

*Although contemporary, this style of
relief carving is similar to Nunivak
Island carving of the 1920's and 1930's.*

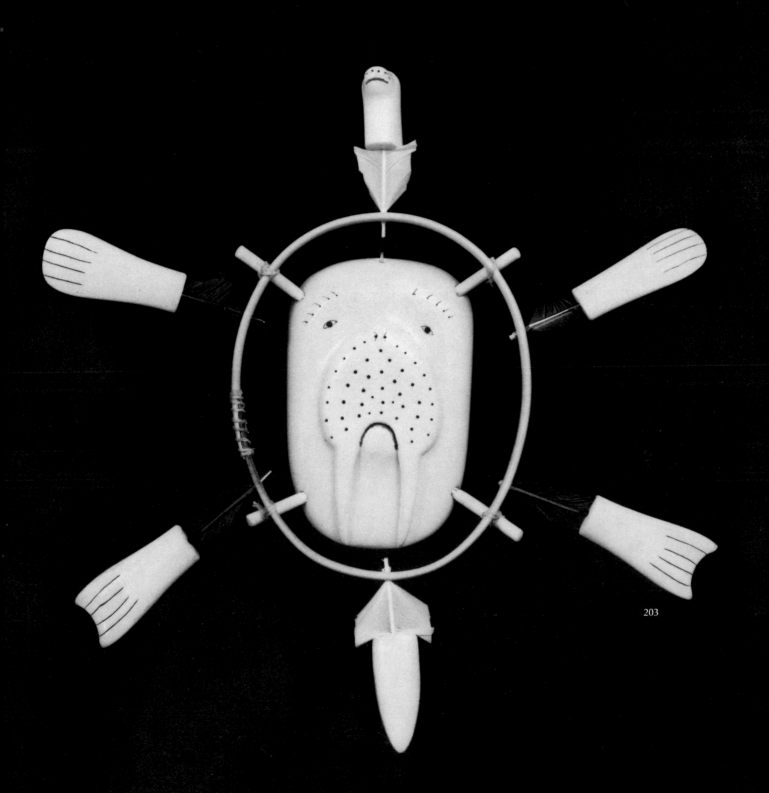

203

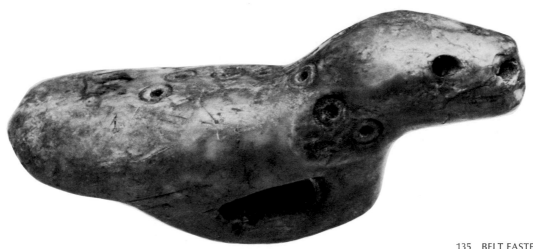

135 BELT FASTENER or CORD
     HANDLE
Walrus ivory in shape of a seal,
incised circle design.
2" (5.1 cm.) long
Newark Museum; 00.313

167 TOBACCO QUID BOX
Wood stained red representing a
walrus skull. The lid is in the shape
of a seal and is hinged with an
ivory pin which serves as the
walrus's eyes. The tusks are made
of walrus ivory.
c. 1920
Cook Inlet
Newark Museum; 21.2040

*Such boxes were used for storing
quids of chewing tobacco.*

62

7

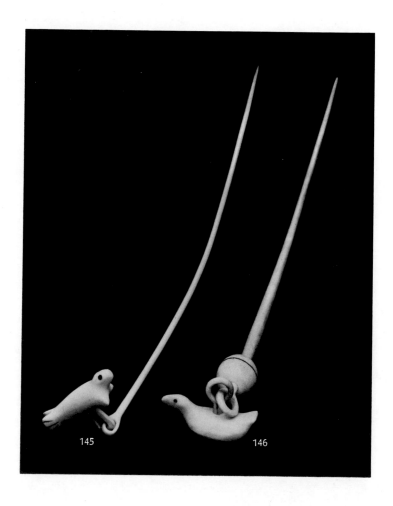

145   146

7   TOGGLE HARPOON
Iron blade held in ivory socket bound
with braided sinew covered with
resin. The animal engraved on the
ivory tip is probably a polar bear.
A bundle of sinew projects from the
back of the harpoon.
13¼" (33.8 cm.) long
Late 19th century
Point Hope
Newark Museum; 21.1508
Possibly used in walrus hunting.

145   HAIRPIN?
Walrus ivory pin with suspended seal
pendant having inlaid baleen eyes.
8¼" (21.2 cm.) long
20th century
Newark Museum; 48.493

146   HAIRPIN?
Walrus ivory pin with suspended duck
pendant having incised eyes.
8½" (21.8 cm.) long
20th century
Newark Museum; 48.494a,b

129 FEMALE DOLL
Bleached sealskin doll dressed in old St. Lawrence Island fashion. The parka is made of walrus gut decorated with cormorant neck feathers and unborn seal around the hem and the cuffs. The hood has a rabbit fur ruff. The doll is wearing sealskin boots with bearded seal *(ugruk)* soles and whale sinew ties. Her hair is braided and adorned with strings of beads.
14½" (36.8 cm.) high
Josephine Ungott, Gambell, St. Lawrence Island
1975
Collection on loan to The Newark Museum

This kind of parka would only have been worn on special occasions, such as during a celebration when the first whale of the spring was caught.

159 DOLL
Wooden head with painted eyes. Parka is of caribou trimmed with beaver and tassels of dog hair. Hood has ruff of wolverine and wolf. Boots are caribou with beaver tops.
14" (35.6 cm.) long
c. 1935
Kuskokwim River
Newark Museum; 38.60

158 DOLL
Bone head with engraved and painted
features. Stuffed body is covered with
checked gingham and is wearing a gut
parka with sealskin trim and sealskin
boots.
10¼" (26.2 cm.) long
Early 20th century
Kuskokwim River
Newark Museum; 38.59

*Carefully crafted toys and dolls as
children's playthings have been made
since prehistoric times. Eskimos are
generally very loving and demonstra-
tive with young children.*

53 WOODBLOCK PRINT
   "ONE CHANCE"
Print on paper in tones of blue and
yellow showing four men in a skinboat
(umiak), one throwing a harpoon into
a large Bowhead Whale.
10½″ (26.7 cm.) diameter, unframed
Bernard Katexac (1922-   )
1974
Collection on loan to
The Newark Museum

Whaling continues as the most important
hunting activity among the Eskimos of
northwest Alaska. Katexac, born on King
Island and now living in Nome, studied
at the University of Alaska's Extension
Center in Arts and Crafts. In addition to
printmaking, he also engraves on ivory.

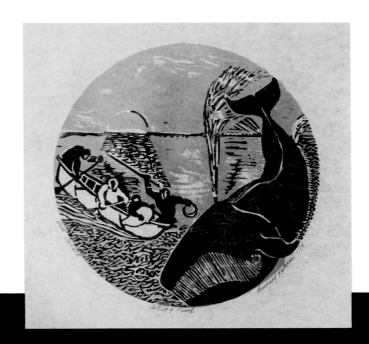

208 PIPE
Walrus ivory with black engraving
showing stylized figures of men and
animals; stone bowl.
10¾″ (27.3 cm.) long
19th century
Western Alaska
Collection on loan to
The Newark Museum

Elaborately carved and engraved 19th
century ivory pipes were not meant to be
smoked but were sold as souvenirs to
Westerners.

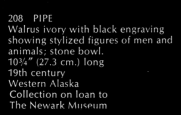

30 SCULPTURE: BEAR
Green soapstone
16½" (41.9 cm.) high
Melvin Olanna (1941-   )
1976
Collection on loan to
The Newark Museum

*Olanna, one of the best-known
contemporary Native artists, has
carved a traditional subject in a
modern, abstract style. Soapstone,
some of which is imported from
outside Alaska, has come into use
among Alaskan Eskimos just the
last few years.*

61 BALEEN BASKET WITH LID
Baleen woven in shades from
white to grey to black, ivory
circle base, ivory walrus as
handle of lid.
4½" high x 8" diameter
(11.5 cm. x 20.3 cm. diameter)
Carl Hank Sr. (1910-   ), Barrow
1972
Anchorage Historical and Fine Arts
Museum; 72.56

*Baleen basket making is a dying
art. Long strips of baleen hang
from the mouths of Bowhead and
other baleen whales through
which they strain their food. The
large pieces of baleen are prepared for basket-making by peel-
ing off the white gum at the
bottom and scraping them clean.
They are then cut lengthwise into
thin strips and the strips are again
scraped and soaked in water to
make them pliable before weav-
ing. The basket is begun around a
flat piece of ivory with holes
drilled around the edges and the
strips are woven in and out with
another strip overlapping the
weave. Baleen scrapings are sometimes used to line the soles
of boots.*

24 CROUCHING HUNTER
     HOLDING SPEAR
Walrus ivory
2½" (5.7 cm.) overall length
Earl Mayac
1976
Collection on loan to
The Newark Museum

*This exquisite figurine is miniature
in size but monumental in its
proportions. The natural variation
in the color of the ivory is beautifully incorporated into the form.
Earl Mayac was born on King
Island but now lives in Anchorage.*

207 SCULPTURE: TWO RAVENS
Green soapstone with incised
drawing
9" x 6½" (22.9 cm. x 16.5 cm.)
Sylvester Ayek
Mid-1970's
Collection on loan to
The Newark Museum

*The drawing shows a shaman with
a raven's head and a drum. He is
doing the raven dance.*

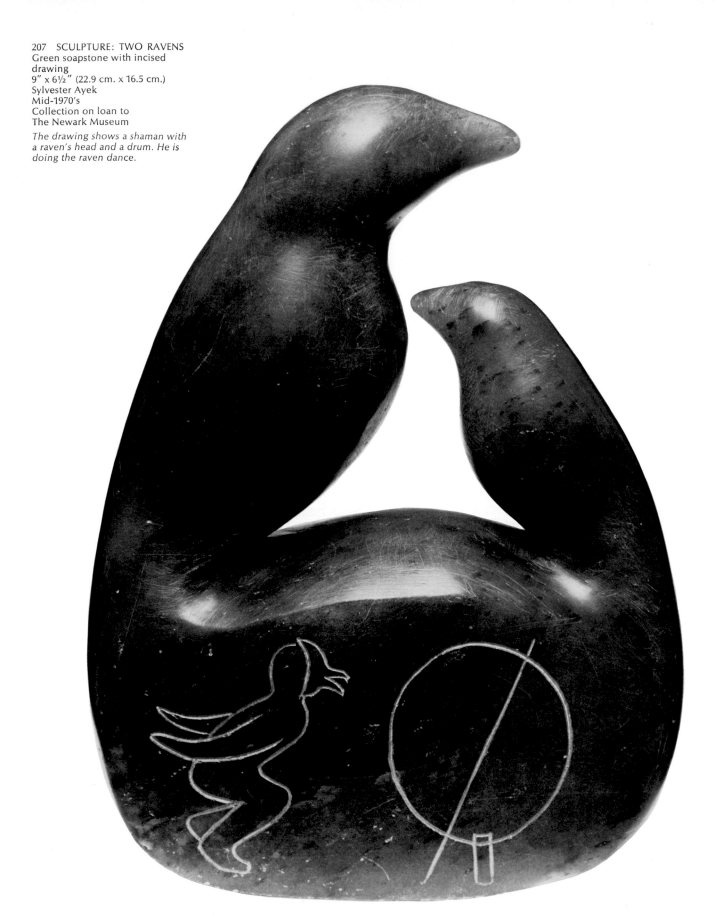

24 CROUCHING HUNTER
    HOLDING SPEAR *Photograph p. 69*
Walrus ivory
2½" (5.7 cm.) overall length
Earl Mayac
1976
Collection on loan to
    The Newark Museum

25 EYE SHADE
Wood, leather
8" (20.3 cm.) wide
c. 1935
Kuskokwim River
Collection of W. R. Olsen, Bethel
Newark Museum; 38.73

26 MODEL OF TWO HOLE KAYAK
    WITH TWO FIGURES
Wood, sealskin, gut, cloth, ivory,
    cotton string. Design painted along
    side of boat is a mythical crocodile-
    like animal known as *pal-raí-yûk*.
22⅛" (56.2 cm.) long
Newark Museum; 48.495

27 KAYAK PADDLE
Wood painted black with incised
    lines and circles, mended with
    sinew
54⅜" (138 cm.) long
19th or early 20th century
Newark Museum; 32.513

28 MALE LOON *Photograph p. 43*
Walrus ivory with black engraving,
    yellow beak
3" (7.6 cm.) long
Peter Mayac (c. 1908-   ),
    Anchorage
1973
Collection on loan to
    The Newark Museum

29 EAGLE *Photograph p. 43*
Walrus ivory with black engraving,
    yellow feet and beak
3⅛" (7.9 cm.) long
Peter Mayac (c. 1908-   ),
    Anchorage
1973
Collection on loan to
    The Newark Museum

30 SCULPTURE: BEAR
    Photograph p. 68
Green soapstone
16½" (41.9 cm.) high
Melvin Olanna (1941-   )
1976
Collection on loan to
    The Newark Museum
*Olanna, one of the best-known con-
temporary Native artists, has carved
an ancient subject in a modern,
abstract style.*

31 SCULPTURE: WALRUS ON ITS
    BACK
Grey field stone
8½" (21.6 cm.) high
Nick Wongitillin, St. Lawrence Island
1964-65
Alaska State Museum, Juneau;
    II-A-4295C

32 POLAR BEAR
Walrus ivory
5⅜" (13.7 cm.) long
Punuk? (c. 1000 A.D.)
Kukulik, St. Lawrence Island.
    Collected by Otto Geist in 1931.
Alaska State Museum, Juneau;
    II-A-3597
*This bear was probably a hunting
charm.*

33 POLAR BEAR
Walrus ivory, inlaid baleen eyes
5¼" (13.34 cm.) long
Mid-1950's
Savoonga, St. Lawrence Island?
Collection on loan to
    The Newark Museum
*Although not carved as a hunting
charm, this bear is almost exactly
similar to the one that was made
perhaps a thousand years earlier.*

34 SEAL
Walrus ivory covered with black
    engraving, baleen eyes
4¾" (12.1 cm.) long
Lincoln Milligrock (1931-   ), Nome
1976
Collection on loan to
    The Newark Museum

35 DOUBLE SEALS
Walrus ivory
5" (12.6 cm.) high; 1⅞" (4.9 cm.) wide
St. Lawrence Island. Collected by
    Otto Geist.
University of Alaska Museum, Fair-
    banks; 1-1934-1873G

36 MARMOT
Wood
7½" (19.1 cm.) high
20th century?
Newark Museum; 48.491

37 PAINTING: CARIBOU ON THE
    SNOW
Watercolor on caribou skin
3¾" x 10" (9.5 cm. x 25.4 cm.)
    unframed
George Ahgupuk (1911-   ),
    Anchorage
Early 1970's
Collection on loan to
    The Newark Museum

38 PAINTING: MOOSE IN
    WOODED AREA
Watercolor on caribou skin
8" x 10" (20.3 cm. x 25.4 cm.)
    unframed
George Ahgupuk (1911-   ),
    Anchorage
Early 1970's
Collection on loan to
    The Newark Museum

39 PRINT: WALRUSES
Woodcut on paper in tones of blue,
    yellow, brown and black showing
    group of 8 walruses crowded
    together on the ice
11½" x 18" (29 cm. x 45.7 cm.)
Bernard Katexac (1922-   ), Nome
1969
Anchorage Historical and Fine Arts
    Museum; 70.152.6

40 PRINT: ENVIRONMENT "2"
Woodcut on paper showing seals in
    an abstract pattern
17⅜" x 23" (44.1 cm. x 58.4 cm.)
Peter Seeganna (1938-1974)
1969
Anchorage Historical and Fine Arts
    Museum; 71.197.1
*Seeganna, whose family was from
King Island, was born and lived in
Nome. He was active as a sculptor,
printmaker and art teacher until his
death. He was given a retrospective
exhibition at The Anchorage His-
torical and Fine Arts Museum,
January-February, 1975.*

41 DRAWING: DOG SLED TEAM
Ink on paper
12" x 18" (30.5 cm. x 45.1 cm.)
Florence Napuk (or Nupok)
    Malewotkuk (c. 1905-1971)
Anchorage Historical and Fine Arts
    Museum; 71.216.1
*Florence Malewotkuk was born and
raised in Gambell on St. Lawrence
Island. During the Otto Geist expedition for the University of Alaska in
1927-28, she drew for him many
pictures recording life on the Island
which are part of the University's
collections. Her best works are large
ink drawings on stretched animal
skins.*

42 SEAL DECOY HELMET
Wood painted white, red and black;
    rawhide strap
10" (25.4 cm.) long
19th century
Kodiak Island. Collected by Edward
    G. Fast, 1867-68.
Peabody Museum, Harvard University;
    69-30-10/64700
Exhibited in "The Far North" 1973-74

43 THROWING BOARD
Wood, ivory
19⅛" (48.6 cm.) long
19th century
Kodiak Island. Collected by Edward
 G. Fast, 1867-68.
Peabody Museum, Harvard University;
 69-30-10/1715
Exhibited in "The Far North" 1973-74

44 THREE SNOW BIRDS
Walrus ivory with black engraving
2¼"-2½" (5.7 cm.-6.4 cm.) high
Aloysius Pikonganna, Nome
1976
Collection on loan to
 The Newark Museum

WHALING

45 WHALE HARPOON HANDREST
Walrus ivory with incised decoration
4" (10.2 cm.) long
Punuk (c. 1000 A.D.)
Collected at Merukhta, St. Lawrence
 Island, 1950's.
Anonymous loan

*Attached to harpoon shaft to give
hand momentum and to keep hand
from slipping while throwing
harpoon.*

46 BOWHEAD WHALE
Walrus ivory
5" (12.7 cm.) long
Punuk? (c. 1000 A.D.)
Collected at Seklowaghyaget,
St. Lawrence Island, end 1950's.
Anonymous loan

47 BOWHEAD WHALE
Walrus ivory, inlaid baleen eyes
5" (12.7 cm.) long
Harry Koozaata (1928-   ), Gambell,
 St. Lawrence Island
Mid-1970's
Collection on loan to
 The Newark Museum

48 UNIDENTIFIED OBJECT WITH
 WHALE'S FLUKES
 Photograph p. 60
Walrus ivory
7½" (19.1 cm.) long
Punuk (c. 1000 A.D.)
Excavated by Vivian Iyakitan on the
 south side of St. Lawrence Island
 about 25 miles from Gambell
Collection on loan to
 The Newark Museum

49 KILLER WHALE
 Photograph p. 14
Walrus ivory with black engraving
6" (15.2 cm.) long
Peter Mayac (c. 1908-   ), Anchorage
1973
Collection on loan to
 The Newark Museum

50 PAINTING: PREPARATION OF
 WALRUS HIDE
Watercolor on paper
17¾" x 22" (45 cm. x 56 cm.) unframed
Diana Tillion, Halibut Cove
1975
Collection of the artist
*This and the following painting were
based on the artist's personal
observation and information received
from the Eskimos at Gambell, St.
Lawrence Island. Walrus are especially
plentiful in the spring in the region of
St. Lawrence Island. The hide is
prepared and split and then sewed to
cover the skin boats used for whaling
and sea mammal hunting.*

51 PAINTING: ALICE SPLITTING
 WALRUS HIDES
Watercolor on paper
14" x 22" (35.5 cm. x 56 cm.) unframed
Diana Tillion, Halibut Cove
1975
Collection of the artist

52 PRINT: YESTERDAY'S SEASONS
Woodcut on paper in red ochre and
 black ink showing Eskimo whalers
 in an *umiak*, a three masted whaling ship, two Bowhead Whales and
 a Killer Whale against a background
 of newspaper headlines.
12⅜" x 22¼" (31.4 cm. x 56.5 cm.)
Joseph Senungetuk (1940-   )
1973
Anchorage Historical and Fine Arts
 Museum; 73.97.3

53 PRINT: ONE CHANCE
 Photograph p. 66
Woodcut on paper
10½" (26.7 cm.) diameter, unframed
Bernard Katexac (1922-   ), Nome
1974
Collection on loan to
 The Newark Museum

54 MASK
Whalebone
7" (18 cm.) high
20th century?
Probably Point Barrow region
Field Museum of Natural History;
 177289
Shown at The Newark Museum only

55 MASK
Wood
15" (38 cm.) high
19th century
Point Hope
Field Museum of Natural History;
 53458

*Characteristic form of whaling mask
showing the animal's mouth and
breathing hole in the mouth and chin
area of a human face. The human
nose is formed by the whale's flukes.*

Shown at The Newark Museum only

56 LID OF BOX USED TO HOLD
 WHALING CHARMS
Wood with carved figure of a whale
8¾" x 12.2" (22 cm. x 31 cm.) long
19th century
Point Hope
Field Museum of Natural History;
 53423

*A small piece of chipped quartz set in
the underside of the lid was a personal charm of the whaler believed
to assist him in hunting and to pro-
tect him from danger.*

Shown at The Newark Museum only

57 HARPOON ICE PICK
Walrus ivory with engraved whaling
 scenes
16⅞" (43 cm.) long
19th century
Western Alaska
Field Museum of Natural History;
 13808

*The ice pick was attached to the
lower end of a harpoon shaft and was
used to test thin ice.*

Shown at The Newark Museum only

58 HARPOON RACK
Walrus ivory with ivory chains,
 carved bears' heads and whales
Approximately 8" (19.3 cm.)
19th century
Sledge Island. Collected by W. B.
 Van Valin in 1916.
University Museum, Philadelphia;
 NA 4796

59 MODEL OF UMIAK WITH
 FIGURES
Wood frame covered with sealskin
 lashed to frame with sealskin
 thong
21" (53.4 cm.) long
Early 1970's
Newark Museum; 76.13a-c

60 TOGGLE-HEAD HARPOON
    FROM A DARTING GUN
Iron
38¼'' (97.2 cm.) long
20th century
East Hampton Town Marine Museum

*The darting gun was introduced by
white whalers to the Eskimos in the
second half of the 19th century. It is
still in use today.*

61 BASKET WITH LID
    Photograph p. 69
Baleen woven in shades from white to
    grey to black, ivory circle base,
    ivory walrus as handle of lid
4½" high x 8" diameter (11.5 cm. x
    20.3 cm. diameter)
Carl Hank Sr. (1910-   ), Barrow
1972
Anchorage Historical and Fine Arts
    Museum; 72.56

FISHING

62 MINIATURE ICE SCOOP
Wood painted with red bands, horn
    scoop with sinew mesh tied with
    string to the handle
12" (30.5 cm.) long
20th century?
Newark Museum; 48.490

*Ice scoops are used to clear ice away
from the hole through which fish
are caught.*

63 ICE FISHING OUTFIT
Notched wooden stick, cotton cord
    line with bone sinker, iron hook
    attached to sinker, red wool
    wrapped around hook
14¾" (37.6 cm.) length of rod
c. 1935
Kuskokwim River
Collection of W. R. Olsen, Bethel
Newark Museum; 38.71 a-c

64 MESH GAUGE FOR MAKING
    NETS
Walrus ivory
6½" (16.6 cm.) long
19th or early 20th century
Newark Museum; 14.238

65 SHUTTLE FOR MAKING NETS
Walrus ivory, sinew
7⅝" (19.5 cm.) long
19th or early 20th century
Kotzebue Sound
Newark Museum; 14.221

66 FISH HOOK
Ivory shank, iron barb, sinew line
1½" (3.9 cm.) length of shank
19th or early 20th century
Newark Museum; 32.705

67 FISH HOOK AND SINKER
Bone sinker, copper wire loops,
    braided hair line dyed red, copper
    hook
4½" (11.6 cm.) length of sinker
20th century?
Kobuk River
Newark Museum; 23.1505

68 FISHING BOB
Wood painted red and black, sinew
6¾" (17.2 cm.) long
19th or early 20th century
Newark Museum; 19.404

69 FISH BREAKER OR KNIFE
Bone, leather
20½" (52 cm.) long
19th or early 20th century
Newark Museum; 19.402

*Such implements were used to pry
frozen fish from the pile in which they
were kept until needed.*

70 FISH ARROW
Painted wood, serrated ivory prongs,
    cotton thread and string
30½" (77.6 cm.) long
20th century
Kuskokwim River
Collection of W. R. Olsen, Bethel
Newark Museum; 38.81

71 FISH TRAP MODEL FOR
    CATCHING BLACKFISH
Willow
15¼" (38.8 cm.) long
c. 1935
Kuskokwim Region
Collection of W. R. Olsen, Bethel
Newark Museum; 38.56 a-c

72 FISH SPEAR
Painted wood shaft, three serrated
    bone points lashed to shaft with
    string
65½" (166.2 cm.) long
20th century
Kuskokwim River
Collection of W. R. Olsen, Bethel
Newark Museum; 38.82

73 DART HEAD FOR SPEARING
    SALMON
Caribou antler
3⅝" (9.2 cm.) long
Arctic Woodland Eskimo
    (c. 1300 A.D.)
Onion Portage. Collected 1960's.
Haffenreffer Museum of Anthro-
    pology, Brown University; 64-1438

74 SHEE FISH HOOK WITH BARB
Walrus ivory, metal hook, brass eyes
3⅝" (9.1 cm.) without barb
1950's
Selawik
Collection of Douglas D. Anderson

75 SHANK OF SHEE FISH HOOK
Walrus ivory
3" (7.7 cm.) long
Arctic Woodland Eskimo
    (c. 1400 A.D.)
Onion Portage. Collected 1960's.
Haffenreffer Museum of Anthro-
    pology, Brown University; 64-2453

76 FISH HOOK
Walrus ivory
1¾" (4.5 cm.) long
University of Alaska Museum, Fair-
    banks; UA76-150-17

77 BAG *Photograph p. 24*
Salmon skin, fish skin, spring mink,
    beads, reindeer hair
6" x 7" (15.3 cm. x 17.8 cm.)
c. 1935
Kuskokwim River
Collection of W. R. Olsen, Bethel
Newark Museum; 38.70

78 BAG
Salmon and fish skin, sinew thread
6¾" x 8½" (17.3 cm. x 21.7 cm.)
20th century
Tikchik Lake?
Newark Museum; 32.370

HOME

79 MODEL OF SIBERIAN STYLE
    HOUSE FROM ST. LAWRENCE
    ISLAND
Wood, sealskin, grass
12¾" (32.4 cm.) high
Soong-ah-rook (phonetic spelling of
    Eskimo name)
20th century
Anchorage Historical and Fine Arts
    Museum; 72.73.8

*This type of house was used for
winter quarters. The sides and support
poles would be of driftwood and the
roof of split hide from female walruses. The house had an inner room
constructed of poles and thatched
tundra grass lined with reindeer
skins. This type of house was used
from approximately 1880 until the
1930's. Previous to 1880, the winter
houses were made of sod and half
buried in the ground.*

80 SEAL OIL LAMP
Stone
Discovered on the southeastern part
  of the Kenai Peninsula near Seward,
  Alaska, c. 1920
University Museum, Philadelphia;
  NA 9251

Seal oil was burned in lamps to pro-
vide light and heat for the homes.
The warmth provided by a single lamp
was sufficient to keep the interior
of the house extremely cozy during
the coldest winter months. The lamp
was the focal point of any Eskimo
home and it was the task of the
Eskimo women to make sure the
flame was kept burning.

81 LAMP
Clay; mixture of blood, hair and earth
4½" (11.5 cm.) diameter
20th century
Collection of W. R. Olsen, Bethel
Newark Museum; 38.83

Used with Spirit Lamp (Newark
Museum 38.84).

82 SPIRIT LAMP
Clay
1¼" (3.4 cm.) diameter
20th century
Collection of W. R. Olsen, Bethel
Newark Museum; 38.84

This small lamp was believed to hold
the spirit of the larger one (Newark
Museum 38.83).

83 STONEWARE POT AND LID
Clay, brownish-red glaze; two carved
  ivory seals on lid
10½" (26.7 cm.) high
1970's
Nelson Island School of Design,
  Toksook Bay
Collection on loan to
  The Newark Museum

The shape has evolved from some of
the old berry baskets and cooking
pots found along the Bering Sea coast.
The clay was obtained along the
coast of Nelson Island close to the
village of Toksook Bay. The reddish
glaze contains calcined walrus bones.
The ivory seals were carved by one of
the men from Toksook Bay village.

84 GUT SCRAPER
Walrus ivory with incised decoration
4½" (10.4 cm.) long
Okvik (c. 0 A.D.)
St. Lawrence Island
Collection on loan to
  The Newark Museum

This piece carries the characteristic
Okvik design motifs of slightly
curved, incised lines with spurred
lines attached, combined with an
occasional circle. It was used to
scrape the fat from intestines.

85 BUCKET HANDLE AND CHAIN
    Photograph p. 22
Walrus ivory with incised decoration
7⅞" (20.02 cm.) long without chain.
  Chain 3⅜" (8.58 cm.) long
Old Bering Sea (c. 500 A.D.)
Collected at Miyowagh, St. Lawrence
  Island, 1950's
Anonymous loan

86 SPOON *Photograph p. 52*
Wood painted with red and black
  design
10⅛" (25.9 cm.) long
c. 1920
Cape York
Newark Museum; 21.2041

87 SPOON *Photograph p. 53*
Musk ox horn with black engraving
  around outer edge
8⅝" (22 cm.) long
19th century
Newark Museum; 32.552

88 SPOON
Musk ox horn with incised lines on
  handle
8⅞" (22.6 cm.) long
Newark Museum; 32.428

89 BERRY PAIL
Wood, spruce root
5¼" (13.5 cm.) high
20th century
Kuskokwim River
Collection of W. R. Olsen, Bethel
Newark Museum; 38.117

90 DISH *Photograph p. 16*
Spruce wood painted red and black
6⅜" (16.3 cm.) long
c. 1935
Kuskokwim River
Collection of W. R. Olsen, Bethel
Newark Museum; 38.51

91 DISH *Photograph p. 52*
Spruce wood painted red and black
8¾" (22.4 cm.) long
c. 1935
Kuskokwim River
Collection of W. R. Olsen, Bethel
Newark Museum; 38.50

92 BOWL
Wood
16" (40.7 cm.) long
20th century
Collection of W. R. Olsen, Bethel
Newark Museum; 38.114

93 FOOD BOWL
Spruce wood, willow, spruceroot
5⅞" (15 cm.) long
20th century?
Newark Museum; 32.565

94 WOMAN'S KNIFE *(ULU)* BLADE
Ground slate
4⅜" (11.1 cm.) long
Arctic Woodland Eskimo
  (c. 1300 A.D.)
Onion Portage. Collected in 1960's.
Haffenreffer Museum of Anthro-
  pology, Brown University; 64-1413

95 WOMAN'S KNIFE *(ULU)*
    HANDLE
Walrus ivory with incised decoration
3⅜" (8.58 cm.) long
Old Bering Sea (c. 500 A.D.)
Collected at Miyowagh, St. Lawrence
  Island, 1950's
Anonymous loan

An ulu is a woman's crescent shaped
knife. It has existed in approximately
the same shape for thousands of
years.

96 CHIPPED *ULU* BLADE
Chert (a flint-like rock)
4½" (11.5 cm.) long
Choris (c. 1500 B.C.)
Onion Portage. Collected in 1960's.
Haffenreffer Museum of Anthro-
  pology, Brown University; 67-6239

Earlier counterpart of modern ulu.
Probably used for cutting fish.

97 WOMAN'S KNIFE *(ULU)*
Bone handle, slate blade
3" (7.8 cm.) wide
Pre-19th century
Newark Museum; 00.266

98 WOMAN'S KNIFE *(ULU)*
Wooden handle painted red and blue;
    slate blade
4" (10.1 cm.) wide
20th century?
Kuskokwim River?
Collection of W. R. Olsen, Bethel
Newark Museum; 38.74

99 NEEDLE CASE
Walrus ivory
19th century? Collected by G. B.
    Gordon, 1915
University Museum, Philadelphia;
    NA 3240

*There is a great variety of form and
materials in these sometimes
ornately and beautifully decorated
cases used to store needles.*

100 NEEDLE CASE
Bird bone with wooden stopper. Tube
    is decorated with etched lines
    darkened red.
3⅞" (9.9 cm.) long
Early 20th century
Kodiak Island
Newark Museum; 14.224 a,b

101 BAG
Gut sewn with cotton thread, seams
    decorated with loops of cotton
    floss, top edged with band of
    feathers and small strips of
    birdskin.
16" x 11½" (40.6 cm. x 29.4 cm.)
20th century?
Newark Museum; 32.368

102 BAG *Photograph p. 48*
Swan's foot leather, reindeer hair,
    wool yarn, silk, cotton cord, beads,
    bird quills
6½" x 7¾" (16.6 cm. x 19.7 cm.)
c. 1935
Point Barrow
Collection of W. R. Olsen, Bethel
Newark Museum; 38.66

103 GRASS COMB
Walrus ivory
4¾" (12.1 cm.) high
Gambell, St. Lawrence Island. Col-
    lected by Philip Campbell.
Alaska State Museum, Juneau;
    II-A-4495

*Comb used for combing grasses used
in the soles of boots.*

104 COILED PLAQUE OR MAT
Salt water grass with geometric
    design of blue, brown and red
    dyed grass
11" (28 cm.) diameter
20th century
Kuskokwim region
Collection of W. R. Olsen, Bethel
Newark Museum; 38.118

105 BASKET
Grass with design of six-legged, blue
    insects
15" (38.1 cm.) high
Julie Simons, Nightmute, Nelson Is.
Early 1970's
Anchorage Historical and Fine Arts
    Museum; 71.160

106 BASKET WITH LID
Grass with red and green butterfly
    design
8" (20.3 cm.) high
Lillian Smith, Hooper Bay,
    Kuskokwim-Yukon Delta region
Early 1970's
Anchorage Historical and Fine Arts
    Museum; 71.29.2

107 BASKET WITH LID
Photograph p. 67
Wild rye grass, walrus hide, beads
4½" (11.5 cm.) high
20th century?
Diomede Islands
Newark Museum; 42.560

108 BASKET
Grass, band of dark blue thread, geo-
    metric designs of brown and blue
    dyed plant fiber
6" (15.3 cm.) high
Early 20th century
Point Barrow
Newark Museum; 20.253

109 BASKET WITH LID
Grass with vertical designs in red and
    blue thread, plant fiber. Handle is
    missing from lid.
7" (17.8 cm.) high
Early 20th century
Point Barrow
Newark Museum; 14.247 a,b

110 FUR RUG
Concentric squares of seal, polar bear
    fur
28" x 28" (71.2 cm. x 71.2 cm.)
20th century?
Newark Museum; 26.770

111 WEDGE?
Engraved caribou antler
6⅜" (16 cm.) long
Arctic Woodland Eskimo
    (1300-1400 A.D.)
Onion Portage. Collected 1960's.
Haffenreffer Museum of Anthro-
    pology, Brown University; 64-2456

112 FIRE KINDLER
Wood, rawhide, ivory handles on
    drill cord. Mouthpiece cap has
    carved animal face on one end.
Stick: 13¼" (33.8 cm.) long; Fire stick:
    5⅜" (13.9 cm.) long; Mouthpiece:
    5⅛" (13.2 cm.) long; Cord 21½"
    (54.6 cm.) long
Early 20th century?
Newark Museum; 19.244 a-e

113 AWL
Bone
7⅝" (19.5 cm.) long
Late 19th or early 20th century
Kuskokwim River
Collection of W. R. Olsen, Bethel
Newark Museum; 38.101

114 FAT SCRAPER
Bone decorated with incised lines
4¾" (12 cm.) long
19th or early 20th century
Newark Museum; 32.746

115 BREAST YOKE
Wood
16¼" (41.3 cm.) long
c. 1935
Kuskokwim River
Collection of W. R. Olsen, Bethel
Newark Museum; 38.55

116 ROOT PICK
Wood, leather, antler
12½" (32 cm.) length of handle
c. 1920
Kuskokwim region
Newark Museum; 21.2039

117 WOODCARVING KNIFE
Bone handle, steel blade, wood,
    spruce root
7⅜" (18.8 cm.) long
Late 19th or early 20th century
Kuskokwim River
Collection of W. R. Olsen, Bethel
Newark Museum; 38.94

118 TOOL CHEST AND COVER
Wood, ivory decorations
21⅛" (53.6 cm.) long
19th century? Collected by Samuel
    Cabot.
Peabody Museum, Harvard University;
    45-28-10/27700

CLOTHING AND ADORNMENT

119 MAN'S PARKA
Squirrel skin parka with reindeer,
  wolverine, beaver, otter, red wool
  yarn and cotton cloth; wolf and
  arctic hare ruff
57½" (146 cm.) long
c. 1924
St. Lawrence Island
Worn by Edward Michael (Ikwa) of
  Bethel, Alaska, when he visited
  Newark in 1934.
Newark Museum; 34.179

120 CHILD'S PARKA
Squirrel skin parka with otter, reindeer, wolf, wolverine, red wool
  yarn, beads; wolverine and wolf ruff
22½" (57.4 cm.) long
c. 1935
Kuskokwim River
Collection of W. R. Olsen, Bethel
Newark Museum; 38.69

121 GUT PARKA
Seal intestine parka, walrus stomach
  under arms, red wool yarn and
  wolverine hair decorations, grass
  stitching
43¼" (109.9 cm.) long
1970's
Kuskokwim region
Newark Museum; 76.11

122 PARKA COVER (KUSPUK)
Cotton flour sacks, rickrack and bias
  tape trim
36½" (92.8 cm.) long
1970's
Noorvik
Newark Museum; 76.12

123 DOLL'S PARKA
    Photograph p. 23
Black throated loon skins, beaver
  trim, blue wool yarn
11½" (29.3 cm.) long
c. 1935
Kuskokwim River
Collection of W. R. Olsen, Bethel
Newark Museum; 38.67

124 BOOTS
Sealskin, bearded seal (ugruk) soles
10¾" (27.4 cm.) long
c. 1935
King Island
Collection of W. R. Olsen, Bethel,
  Alaska
Newark Museum; 38.64 a,b

125 BOOTS
Reindeer, wolverine, dog, wool, yarn,
  beads; sealskin soles
10⅝" (27 cm.) long
c. 1924
Worn by Edward Michael (Ikwa) of
  Bethel, Alaska, when he visited
  Newark in 1934.
Newark Museum; 34.180 a,b

126 CHILD'S BOOTS
Sealskin
6⅜" (16.4 cm.) long
Early 20th century
St. Michael?
Newark Museum; 32.362

127 BELT
Rawhide sewn with rows of caribou
  teeth, beads, brass disks
51¾" (131.6 cm.) long
Early 20th century
Kuskokwim River
Collection of W. R. Olsen, Bethel
Newark Museum; 38.62

*Such belts were worn outside their
parkas by women and indicated a
successful hunter in the family,
since each row of teeth represents
one caribou killed.*

128 MITTENS
Caribou
11¾" (30 cm.) long
c. 1935
Kuskokwim River
Collection of W. R. Olsen, Bethel
Newark Museum; 38.63 a,b

129 SEALSKIN PANTS
Spotted seal lined with cotton cloth,
  skins sewn with sinew
32" (81.13 cm.) long
Early 20th century
St. Lawrence Island
Collected by Otto Geist in the late
  1920's.
University of Alaska Museum,
  Fairbanks; UA66-2-52

130 MALE AND FEMALE DOLLS
    DRESSED IN OLD ST.
    LAWRENCE ISLAND FASHION
    Photograph p. 64
Bleached sealskin dolls, walrus gut
  parkas with cormorant neck
  feathers, rabbit fur, unborn seal;
  sealskin boots with bearded seal
  (ugruk) soles and whale sinew ties.
  Male wears sealskin trousers.
Male: 15½" (39.4 cm.) high;
  female: 14½" (36.8 cm.) high
Josephine Ungott, Gambell,
  St. Lawrence Island
1975
Collection on loan to
  The Newark Museum

131 ARMOR PLATE
Four pieces of copper lashed with
  thong
3¾" (9.3 cm.) high; 4½" (14.2 cm.)
  wide
19th century
Kukulik, St. Lawrence Island
University of Alaska Museum,
  Fairbanks; 1-1935-8749

*Armor was sometimes made from
plates of ivory or bone. Its use was
common during warfare among the
people living throughout the Bering
Strait region during the Punuk period
and later. Copper armor plate came
into use about 1850.*

132 HAIR COMB
Antler with incised geometric designs
3" (7.5 cm.) high
Collected by Lt. G. T. Emmons.
Alaska State Museum, Juneau;
  II-A-1155
*Such combs were used by both males
and females.*

133 BROW BAND?
Bone semi-circular band with a hole
  on either end probably to insert
  thong
3½" (8.9 cm.) diameter across
  opening
Punuk (c. 1000 A.D.)
Excavated by Vivian Iyakitan on the
  south side of St. Lawrence Island
  about 25 miles from Gambell
Collection on loan to
  The Newark Museum

134 BELT FASTENER Photograph p. 30
Walrus ivory
2⅜" (6.04 cm.) long
Old Bering Sea (c. 500 A.D.)
Collected at Miyowagh, St. Lawrence
  Island, 1950's
Anonymous loan

135 BELT FASTENER Photograph p. 62
Walrus ivory in shape of seal, incised
  circle design
2" (5.1 cm.) long
Newark Museum; 00.313

136 STRING OF TRADE BEADS
Glass and china beads, cotton thread
3" (7.7 cm.) diameter
Mid-19th century
Kuskokwim River
Collection of W. R. Olsen, Bethel
Newark Museum; 38.104

137 EAR BUTTONS
Pendant of white button, glass beads,
   feather shafts strung on cotton
   thread
3" (7.6 cm.) long
c. 1937
Kuskokwim River
Collection of W. R. Olsen, Bethel
Newark Museum; 38.90 a,b

138 EAR BUTTONS AND BEADS
Ivory buttons etched with concentric
   circles, bead pendants; chain of
   red, white and blue beads which
   passes under the chin, strung on
   cotton
12½" (31.9 cm.) long
20th century
Kuskokwim River
Collection of W. R. Olsen, Bethel
Newark Museum; 38.106

139 EAR BUTTONS
Circular ivory buttons with four
   knob-like projections around edge
½" (1.4 cm.) diameter
20th century
Kuskokwim River
Collection of W. R. Olsen, Bethel
Newark Museum; 38.105 a,b

140 SCULPTURE: HEAD OF
      ST. LAWRENCE ISLAND ESKIMO.
Gray soapstone, walrus ivory labrets
7'' x 8¼'' (17.8 cm. x 21.0 cm.)
Harry Koozaata (Melootka) (1928-),
   Gambell, St. Lawrence Island
1974
Collection on loan to
   The Newark Museum

*Sculpture shows a man's head with
hair cut in a tonsure around a bare
scalp as it was formerly worn on
St. Lawrence Island. He is wearing
labrets in the old fashioned manner.*

141 HUMAN HEAD *Photograph p. 32*
Walrus ivory
2½" (6.5 cm.) high
Old Bering Sea (c. 500 A.D.)
St. Lawrence Island
University of Alaska Museum,
   Fairbanks; 1-1931-961

142 LABRET
Walrus ivory, stud-shaped form
1¼" (3.2 cm.) wide
Newark Museum; 00.344

143 LABRET
Walrus ivory, hat-shaped form
1" (2.5 cm.) wide
Early 20th century
Point Barrow
Newark Museum; 14.229

144 WOMAN'S LABRETS
Walrus ivory, sickle-shaped form
⅞" (2.4 cm.) wide
20th century
Nunivak Island
Collection of W. R. Olsen, Bethel
Newark Museum; 38.85 a-d

145 HAIRPIN? *Photograph p. 63*
Walrus ivory, ivory seal pendant with
   baleen eyes
8¼" (21.2 cm.) long
20th century
Newark Museum; 48.493

146 HAIRPIN? *Photograph p. 63*
Walrus ivory, ivory duck pendant with
   incised eyes
8½" (21.8 cm.)
20th century
Newark Museum; 48.494 a,b

RECREATION

147 FINGER MASKS *Photograph p. 27*
Painted wood, reindeer beard hair,
   arctic owl feathers
4½" (11.5 cm.) height of wood
c. 1935
Kuskokwim River
Collection of W. R. Olsen, Bethel
Newark Museum; 38.348 a,b

148 FINGER MASKS *Photograph p. 58*
Painted wood, reindeer beard hair,
   raven and arctic owl feathers
4¾" (12.1 cm.) height of wood
c. 1935
Kuskokwim River
Collection of W. R. Olsen, Bethel
Newark Museum; 38.349 a,b

149 PAINTING: THE DANCE OF
      KAKAIRNOK
Oil on canvas
29¾" x 23½" (75.6 cm. x 59.7 cm.)
Howard (Weyahok) Rock (1911-1976)
1961
Anchorage Historical and Fine Arts
   Museum; 75.53.1

*Howard Rock, born in Point Hope,
Alaska, was one of the best loved and
most highly respected native leaders
of his time. The painting shows Rock's
brother, Kakairnok, telling his dead
father and mother through dance that
he had caught a whale and how
thankful he was that there would be
meat for the village of Tigara (Point
Hope).*

150 ESKIMO DANCER AND ESKIMO
      DRUMMER
Walrus ivory
Dancer: 2⅜" (6.0 cm.) high; Drummer
   2⅞" (7.3 cm.) high
Herbert Kokuluk
1976
Collection on loan to
   The Newark Museum

151 DANCE FILLET *Photograph p. 58*
Long haired reindeer, summer mink,
   white reindeer, hair seal, flannel,
   calico, yarn
11⅛" (28.3 cm.) wide
c. 1935
Kuskokwim River
Collection of W. R. Olsen, Bethel
Newark Museum; 38.58

152 LUTE *Photograph p. 53*
Painted wood
17⅝" (44.8 cm.) long
c. 1935
Kuskokwim Region
Collection of W. R. Olsen, Bethel
Newark Museum; 38.54

153 GROUP OF FIVE TOY BIRDS
Walrus tooth ivory
4/5" (2.1 cm.) long to 1½" (3.8 cm.)
   long
St. Lawrence Island. Collected by
   Otto Geist.
University of Alaska Museum, Fair-
   banks; 1-1934-1670G; 1-1933-8660G;
   UA76-150-13; UA76-150-14; UA76-
   150-15

Used in the gambling game of Ting-
miujaq *where the birds and other
little figurines were thrown like dice
and those that landed upright won a
point. They were usually strung
together on a thong.*

154 TOY DOUBLE BIRDS
Walrus ivory
1¼" (2.8 cm.) width at back
Kukulik, St. Lawrence Island
University of Alaska Museum, Fair-
   banks; 1-1933-8272G

155 TOY REINDEER AND SLED
Walrus ivory
Deer: 4" (10.2 cm.) long; sled 4¼"
   (10.8 cm.) long
Late 19th or early 20th century
Newark Museum; 14.234 a,b

156 TOY DOG
Wood
10" (26 cm.) long
1920's
St. Lawrence Island. Collected by the
   Bunnell-Geist Bering Sea Expedition
   in 1927.
University of Alaska Museum, Fairbanks; UA76-150-18 (1-1927)

157 BABY DOLL
Wood
9" (23 cm.) long
1920's
St. Lawrence Island. Collected by the
    Bunnell-Geist Bering Sea Expedition
    in 1927.
University of Alaska Museum, Fair-
    banks; 1-1927-495

*The doll is shown in the same
position a real baby would take while
being carried on the mother's back
inside her parka.*

158 DOLL *Photograph p. 65*
Bone, cotton, sealskin, gut
10¼" (26.2 cm.) long
Early 20th century
Kuskokwim River
Collection of W. R. Olsen, Bethel
Newark Museum; 38.59

159 DOLL *Photograph p. 64*
Wood, caribou, beaver, dog, wolf,
    wolverine, cotton
14" (35.6 cm.)
c. 1935
Kuskokwim River
Collection of W. R. Olsen, Bethel
Newark Museum; 38.60

160 DOLL'S BOOTS
Sealskin, gut
2⅞" (7.5 cm.) high
20th century
St. Michael?
Newark Museum; 32.375 a,b

161 BALL
Root, inside rattles
17½" (44.5 cm.) circumference
20th century
Kuskokwim River
Collection of W. R. Olsen, Bethel
Newark Museum; 38.119

162 BALL
Sealskin, caribou, reindeer beard
21¾" (55.5 cm.) circumference
c. 1935
St. Lawrence Island
Collection of W. R. Olsen, Bethel
Newark Museum; 38.65

163 STORY KNIFE *Photograph p. 55*
Walrus ivory with incised decoration
    of lines and dots
13⅜" (34 cm.) long
19th or early 20th century
Kuskokwim River
Collection of W. R. Olsen, Bethel
Newark Museum; 38.338

164 STORY KNIFE
Walrus ivory with black engraved
    lines, red engraved dots
17⅜" (44.1 cm.) long
19th century
Collection on loan to
    The Newark Museum

165 STORY KNIFE
Walrus ivory
6¾" (17.2 cm.) long
19th or early 20th century
Kuskokwim River
Collection of W. R. Olsen, Bethel
Newark Museum; 38.339

166 TOBACCO BOX
Wood
3¼" (8.3 cm.) long
20th century
Kuskokwim River
Collection of W. R. Olsen, Bethel
Newark Museum; 38.107

167 TOBACCO QUID BOX
    Photograph p. 62
Wood stained red, ivory
4⅞" (12. 5 cm.) long
c. 1920
Cook Inlet
Newark Museum; 21.2040

168 TOBACCO QUID BOX
Spruce wood painted red and black,
    ivory
5½" (14 cm.) long
19th or early 20th century
Kuskokwim River
Newark Museum; 14.240

169 DOLL
Walrus ivory with braided hair
3¾" (9.5 cm.) high
Field Museum of Natural History;
    13618

Shown at The Newark Museum only

170 PIPE
Wood, ivory, brass cartridge
9⅞" (25 cm.) long
19th century
Western Alaska
Field Museum of Natural History;
    111687

*In contrast to the elaborately carved
and engraved ivory pipes, this was
intended for use. The pipe bowl held
only one pinch of tobacco and the
entire contents were inhaled at one
time.*

Shown at The Newark Museum only

171 PIPE
Wood, metal
8¾" (22.2 cm.) long
19th or early 20th century
Northwest Siberia. Collected by
    Raymond Emerson.
Peabody Museum, Harvard University;
    31-32-60, D3712

*Siberian style pipes such as this were
also made on St. Lawrence Island,
where most of the Eskimos are of
Siberian ancestry. They still make
these pipes today, although they are
not intended to be smoked.*

172 PIPE
Wood, metal
7¾" (19.7 cm.) long
Vernon Wahiye, St. Lawrence Island
1974
Collection on loan to
    The Newark Museum

*This pipe is made in the ancient
Siberian style.*

RELIGION AND CEREMONY

173 HUMAN FIGURE
Walrus ivory
3⅛" (8 cm.) high
Okvik (c. 0 A.D.)
Punuk Island, Ancient Village Site
University of Alaska Museum, Fair-
    banks; 4-1934-693

174 HUMAN FIGURE
Walrus ivory
4½" (10.9 cm.) high
Okvik (c. 0 A.D.)
Punuk Island, Old Site. Collected by
    Otto Geist in 1931.
University of Alaska Museum, Fair-
    banks; 1-1931-832

175 FEMALE FIGURE
Walrus ivory, 3 incised lines repre-
    senting tattoos on chin
3⅝" (9.2 cm.) high
Collected by Lt. G. T. Emmons.
Alaska State Museum, Juneau;
    I-A-3260b

*There are holes drilled in the top of
the head and a hole drilled through
the head at the ears indicating that
this figurine was probably worn as
a fetish.*

176 FEMALE FIGURE
    Photograph p. 49
Walrus ivory
6¾" (17.2 cm.) high
Okvik (c. 0 A.D.)
Punuk Islands
Collection on loan to The Newark
    Museum

177 MASK *Photograph p. 2*
Painted wood
8½" (21.7 cm.) high
c. 1935
Kuskokwim River
Collection of W. R. Olsen, Bethel
Newark Museum; 38.343 a-c

178 MASK *Photograph p. 58*
Painted wood, reindeer beard hair
12" (30.6 cm.) high
c. 1935
Kuskokwim River
Collection of W. R. Olsen, Bethel
Newark Museum; 38.340

179 MASK *Photograph p. 47*
Wood, ivory, string
8⅜" (21.4 cm.) high
c. 1935
Kuskokwim River
Collection of W. R. Olsen, Bethel
Newark Museum; 38.72

180 MASK *Photograph p. 56*
Stained wood, bird quills
12¼" (31.2 cm.) high
c. 1935
Kuskokwim River
Collection of W. R. Olsen, Bethel
Newark Museum; 38.341 a-f

181 MASK *Photograph p. 57*
Wood, rawhide, resin, string
8½" (21.5 cm.) high
c. 1935
Kuskokwim River
Collection of W. R. Olsen, Bethel
Newark Museum; 38.342

182 GRAVE MASK
    Photograph p. 51
Stained wood, ivory
8⅛" (20.8 cm.) high
20th century?
Kuskokwim River
Collection of W. R. Olsen, Bethel
Newark Museum; 38.347

183 MASK *Photograph p. 50*
Painted wood
9¼" (23.2 cm.) high
c. 1935
Kuskokwim River
Collection of W. R. Olsen, Bethel
Newark Museum; 38.346 a-e

184 DOUBLE MASK
    Photograph p. 46
Painted wood, rawhide
13" (33 cm.) high
c. 1935
Kuskokwim River
Collection of W. R. Olsen, Bethel
Newark Museum; 38.344 a-c

185 DOUBLE MASK
    Photograph p. 46
Stained and painted wood, rawhide,
    bird quills
12¼" (31.2 cm.) long
c. 1935
Kuskokwim River
Collection of W. R. Olsen, Bethel
Newark Museum; 38.345 a-c

186 MASK
Wood painted red, black and white;
    peg teeth
15½" (39.4 cm.) long
19th century. Collected by the Bureau
    of Education of the Interior
    Department.
National Museum of Natural History,
    Smithsonian Institution; 260,549

187 DANCE MASK
Wood and feathers
11¾" (29.9 cm.) high, excluding
    feathers; 15⅜" (39 cm.) wide
19th century. Collected by
    G. B. Gordon, 1907.
Kuskokwim River
University Museum, Philadelphia;
    NA 1555

188 MASK
Wood
6¾" (17.2 cm.) high
19th century
Point Barrow. Collected by
    E. A. McIlhenny in 1910.
University Museum, Philadelphia;
    42367

This is a dance mask known as
A-kar-too, *used to dance on the*
arrival of the new moon.

189 MASK
Wood painted green, interior nostrils
    and mouth red, peg teeth, sealskin
    strip on upper edge of jaw
11⅜" (29 cm.) high; 5¾" (14.5 cm.)
    wide
19th or early 20th century
Hooper Bay Region. Collected by
    W. B. Van Valin, 1917-19, John
    Wanamaker Expedition.
University Museum, Philadelphia;
    NA 10344

190 SEAL MASK
Painted wood in tones of red and
    blue; three circular hoops attached
    by four radii to a central oval disc
    with seal's face. Four carved and
    painted flippers and one tail flap
    attached to central disk; two fish
    pendant from outer hoop.
15" (38 cm.) long; 13¾" (35 cm.) wide
19th or early 20th century
Nunivak Island. Collected by
    W. B. Van Valin, 1917.
University Museum, Philadelphia;
    NA 6384

191 SCULPTURE: MASK MOBILE
Wood and ivory. Mobile consists of
    four centerpieces suspended from
    a wooden frame with two ivory
    appendages attached to the second
    piece from the top and a third
    ivory piece suspended just above
    the bottom piece.
Approximately 36" (91.4 cm.) high
Sylvester Ayek
1974
Anchorage Historical and Fine Arts
    Museum; 75.49.1

This is a completely abstract rendition
of an ancient theme.

192 SCULPTURE: SHAMAN TURN-
    ING INTO SEAL
    Photograph p. 39
Ivory and sterling silver
6" x 6" (15.2 cm. x 15.2 cm.)
Lawrence Ahvakana (1946-   )
1975
Collection of the Visual Arts Center
    of Alaska, Anchorage

193 CHARM
Wooden board painted red with blue
  circle in center. Five ivory seal
  heads in blue circle and one head
  in each corner. Ivory handle with
  engraved cross-hatched decoration
  has hole at end for hanging. Blue
  line across back of board. Pencilled
  inscription on back, "If you hang
  this on the wall your house will
  always have plenty of blubber to
  eat."
8¼" (21 cm.) long
20th century?
Newark Museum; 48.489

194 WATERCOLOR PAINTING:
       SHAMAN AND DEVIL
Watercolor and ink on paper
12¼" x 18¼" (31 cm. x 46.4 cm.)
James (Kivetoruk) Moses (c. 1900-   )
Early 1970's
University of Alaska Museum, Fair-
  banks; UA72-20-1

*A white man with a devil's head pro-
trudes halfway through the opening
in the floor leading into the community house where he is confronted
by an Eskimo shaman. A fully clothed
drummer sits on the floor to the left.*

195 MASK
Painted wood, carved figures
23½" (59.7 cm.) long
19th century
Askinuk Mountain region. Collected
  by I. Albert Lee.
Peabody Museum, Harvard University; 06-25-10/66314

*Too large to be worn, this mask
would hang from the roof of the
ceremonial dance hall.*

MISCELLANEOUS

196 DRILL BOW
Walrus ivory engraved with black
  showing scenes of village life and
  animals.
16½" (41.9 cm.) long
19th century
Alaska State Museum, Juneau; II-A-5

*Engraved drill bows were very char-
acteristic of mid-19th century Alaskan
Eskimo art and provided a picto-
graphic record of daily activities and
surroundings. It is uncertain whether
they were made for the artist's own
use and pleasure or whether they
were designed for the early tourist
trade.*

197 DRILL BOW
Walrus ivory engraved with black
  showing many small figures of
  animals and men engaged in hunting activities. Leather thong
  attached.
17" (43.2 cm.) long
19th century
Alaska State Museum, Juneau; II-A-10
Exhibited at "Century 21" World's
  Fair, Seattle, 1962

198 BOW DRILL
Steel drill mounted in wooden shaft.
  Wooden mouthpiece with ivory
  socket. Bow is undecorated curved
  piece of bone with rawhide thong.
Bow: 15" (38.1 cm.) long; Drill: 9⅛"
  (23.3 cm.) long; Mouthpiece: 2¾"
  (7 cm.) long
Late 19th or early 20th century
Point Barrow
Newark Museum; 14.230 a-c

*Bow drills are used for drilling holes
in ivory.*

199 CRIBBAGE BOARD
    Photograph p. 18/19
Walrus ivory tusk with black
  engraving
23¼" (59.1 cm.) long
"Happy Jack" or Angokwazhuk
  (c. 1870-1918)
Late 19th or early 20th century
Collection on loan to
  The Newark Museum

200 CRIBBAGE BOARD
    Photograph p. 54
Walrus ivory tusk with black engraving, ivory animal figures, additional
  ivory piece saying "Nome Alaska
  1922"
22⅝" (57.6 cm.) long
1922
Nome
Newark Museum; 23.1387 a-h

201 CARVED WALRUS TUSK
Walrus ivory
18" (46.2 cm.) long
1920's-1930's
Nunivak Island. Signed HC on side.
Peabody Museum of Salem; E.41.020

*These extremely beautiful tusks of
intertwined animals are deeply
sculpted in relief. They were made
only on Nunivak Island and are
unique among Eskimo carvings in
style.*

202 CARVED WALRUS TUSK
Walrus ivory showing intertwined
  figures of seals with black and red
  engraved designs
10½" (26.7 cm.) high
1930's
Nunivak Island
Alaska State Museum, Juneau;
  II-A-4738

*This is a finely made carving and
appears to be one of the last of the
pieces made originally in this style.*

203 WALRUS MASK
    Photograph p. 61
Walrus ivory with red and black
  engraving, bird feathers
7⅝" (19.4 cm.) overall height
1970's
Nunivak Island
Collection on loan to
  The Newark Museum

204 WINGED OBJECT
Walrus ivory with incised surface
  designs and a sculptured face and
  head on one side
8″ (20.3 cm.) long
Old Bering Sea III (c. 500 A.D.)
Collected by Captain Joe Bernard,
  early 1900's.
University Museum, Philadelphia;
  NA 4245
Exhibited in "The Far North" 1973-74

*The use of these so-called "winged
objects" is unknown but they may
have been harpoon tailpieces. This
example is particularly fine.*

205 MALE FIGURINE
Walrus ivory
Approximately 4″ tall
Collected by General P. H. Ray, 1915.
University Museum, Philadelphia;
  NA 3259

206 PAINTING: POLAR BEAR AND
  BROWN BEAR FIGHT OVER
  A DEAD WALRUS
  Photograph p. 42
Watercolor and ink on paper
12″ x 18″ (30.5 cm. x 45.7 cm.) unframed
James (Kivetoruk) Moses (c. 1900-   )
Early 1970's
Collection on loan to
  The Newark Museum

207 SCULPTURE: TWO RAVENS
  Photograph p. 70
Green soapstone with incised drawing
  of dancing shaman with raven's
  head and a drum
9″ x 6½″ (22.9 cm. x 16.5 cm.)
Sylvester Ayek
Mid-1970's
Collection on loan to
  The Newark Museum

208 PIPE *Photograph p. 66*
Walrus ivory with black engraving
  showing stylized figures of men
  and animals; stone bowl
10¾″ (27.3 cm.) long
19th century
Western Alaska
Collection on loan to
  The Newark Museum

209 PIPE
Walrus ivory with black engraving
  showing hunting and fishing scenes,
  animals, birds and fish
15½″ (39.5 cm.) long
19th century
Kotzebue area. Collected by Reverend
  Sheldon Jackson.
National Museum of Natural History,
  Smithsonian Institution; 316,793

210 PIPE
Walrus ivory carved with animals
17¾″ (45.1 cm.) long
19th century
St. Michael region. Collected by
  Charles Ashley Weare.
Peabody Museum, Harvard Univer-
  sity; 25-5-10/98153

211 PIPE AND TAMPER (?)
Walrus ivory carved in the shape of
  sea animals
12″ (30.5 cm.) length of pipe
19th century. Collected by Ernest
  Jackson in 1880-1900.
Peabody Museum, Harvard University; 46-78-10/28047

212 ORNAMENTAL BAND?
Incised walrus ivory in the form of a
  bird's head with elongated beak
10½″ (26½ cm.) long
Ipiutak (c. 300 A.D.)
Point Hope. Excavated by Larsen and
  Rainey.
American Museum of Natural History;
  60.2-3970
Illustrated in Plate 51, *Ipiutak and the
  Arctic Whale Hunting Culture,* by
  Larsen and Rainey.

*The Ipiutak culture does not appear
to fall within the continuum of other
Arctic cultures. Ipiutak carving was
very elaborate and refined and is
related in motif and design to Okvik
and Old Bering Sea carvings as well
as to Scytho-Siberian art.*

213 ORNAMENTAL LINKED OBJECT
Walrus ivory
11¾″ (29.7 cm.) long
Ipiutak (c. 300 A.D.)
Point Hope. Excavated by Larsen and
  Rainey.
American Museum of Natural History;
  60.2-4345
Illustrated in Plate 72, *Ipiutak and the
  Arctic Whale Hunting Culture,* by
  Larsen and Rainey.

214 ANIMAL CARVING
Walrus ivory
5⅞″ (15 cm.) high
Ipiutak (c. 300 A.D.)
Point Hope. Excavated by Larsen and
  Rainey
American Museum of Natural History;
  60.1-7580a
Illustrated in Plate 53, *Ipiutak and the
  Arctic Whale Hunting Culture,* by
  Larsen and Rainey

*This anthropomorphic figure suggests
a man-seal with shoulders and arms
of a man and hind flippers of a seal.
It has a wide, flat head with a broad,
open mouth. The reverse side is flat.*

This bibliography offers a selection, from a large literature, of materials chosen and annotated for their pertinence to the art and life of the Alaskan Eskimo. Bibliographies offering further coverage are listed first. Materials on the early explorations, the Russian period, the introduction of the reindeer and travel books are not included. They are covered in Ray, *The Eskimos of Bering Strait* and Wickersham, *A Bibliography of Alaskan Literature.*

Most of the material was selected from the literature of the field of anthropology which includes the archaeological reports on the early cultures, the ethnographic accounts on the historical Eskimo, and the recent publications on cultural change and the adaptation of the Eskimo to the modern world. Oswalt, *Alaskan Eskimos,* gives a complete general summary, with a survey of the literature and a thorough discussion of the problem of Eskimo origins.

The art literature is meager by comparison. Prehistoric and traditional art are covered in general works such as Covarrubias and Haberland, and in the more specialized works of Ray, Swinton and Van Stone. Collins, *Eskimo Cultures,* offers a basic general introduction relying heavily on the anthropological material. Contemporary Eskimo art is especially poorly represented. At a time when Eskimo art is recognized and appreciated, and as opportunities for training and exhibition are increasing for the contemporary Eskimo artist, we may expect fuller representation in the future. It is, therefore, an appropriate time to offer this summary of the present literature, while looking forward to continued and expanded publication as the Eskimos take their place in the modern world of a rapidly changing Alaska.

ALLAN D. CHAPMAN
Museum Librarian,
The Department of Primitive Art
The Metropolitan Museum of Art

Arctic Bibliography, v. 1-16. Washington, D. C., Arctic Institute of North America, 1953-1973.

A basic key to the literature. Begun in 1947 with the U. S. Department of Defense. Henry B. Collins, Chairman of the Directing Committee, Marie Tremaine, editor. Offers a total of 108,000 entries with abstracts by specialists on science, technology and the arts. Each volume is arranged alphabetically by author with a subject and geographical index.

Cavanagh, Beverly. Annotated bibliography: Eskimo music. *Ethnomusicology,* v. 16; 1972: p. 479-487.

". . . works dealing exclusively or extensively with music — traditions and customs, melodic or textual transcriptions and analysis — are cited." Useful for references on musical instruments as well as music.

Dockstader, Frederick J. and Dockstader, Alice W. *The American Indian in Graduate Studies; a Bibliography of Theses and Dissertations,* 2d ed. New York, Museum of the American Indian, Heye Foundation [1973]. 2v. (Contributions from the Museum of the American Indian, Heye Foundation, v. 25, pt. 1-2).

First edition, 1957. Includes the Eskimo. Part 1, a reprint of the first edition. Part 2, a supplement with new index, new introduction and new list of schools. Total of 7446 items listed, often with brief annotations. Indexed by tribe and by subject. Important reference, easier to use than *Dissertation Abstracts,* and most valuable for the inclusion of master's theses.

Harding, Anne D. and Bolling, Patricia. *Bibliography of Articles and Papers on North American Indian Art, compiled . . .* under the direction of Dr. Otto Klineberg in co-operation with Dr. George Vaillant and Dr. W. D. Strong. [Washington, D. C., Department of the Interior, Indian Arts and Crafts Board, 1938]. 365p. map.

Includes the Eskimo. Lists articles in the major anthropological journals by author, with a detailed index to material and technique. A major guide to the older literature.

Harvard University. Peabody Museum of Archaeology and Ethnology, Cambridge, Mass. Library. *Catalogue: Authors.* Boston, Mass., G. K. Hall, 1963. 26v., 3 suppl., 1970-1975, 11v.

Harvard University. Peabody Museum of Archaeology and Ethnology, Cambridge, Mass. Library. *Catalogue: Subjects.* Boston, Mass., G. K. Hall, 1963. 27v., 3 suppl., 1970-1975, 13v.

Printed catalog of one of the major libraries in its field, with extensive holdings on the Eskimo. Includes an index to subject headings. Lists and analyzes all the major works in the field of anthropology. Perhaps the single most valuable source available.

Hippler, Arthur E. *Eskimo Acculturation: a Selected Annotated Bibliography of Alaskan and Other Eskimo Acculturation Studies.* College, Alaska, University of Alaska, 1970. 209p. (University of Alaska, Institute of Social, Economic and Government Research, ISEGR Report, 28).

Covers literature chiefly on northwestern Alaska with some material on Aleut and Siberians for comparison. Arranged by author with an area index. Includes dissertations.

Index to Literature on the American Indian. Editorial board: Jeannette Henry, Helen Redbird-Selam, Mary Nelson, Rupert Costo. [San Francisco, Calif.] Published for the American Indian Historical Society by the Indian Historian Press [1972]-.

An annual publication. Includes the Eskimo. A selective alphabetic listing by author and subject area. Includes a list of topics covered, and a list of periodicals indexed.

Murdock, George P. *Ethnographic Bibliography of North America,* ed. [by] George Peter Murdock and Timothy J. O'Leary, with the assistance of John Beierle [and others]. 4th ed. New Haven, Conn., Human Relations Area Files Press, 1975. 5v. maps (Behavior Science Bibliographies).

First edition, 1941. Long the standard bibliography; the fourth edition has been greatly expanded. Arranged by cultural areas. Volume 2, *Arctic and Subarctic,* 255p., includes an ethnic map and an Arctic-Subarctic Ethnonymy as an index. The general introduction covers archives, documents and reference books not included in the Bibliography.

New York. New York Public Library. American History Division. *Dictionary Catalog of the History of the Americas.* Boston, Mass., G. K. Hall, 1961. 28v.

Printed catalog of a major collection with extensive holdings on the Eskimo and on the history of Alaska. A dictionary catalog arranged by author and by subject headings with cross-references.

Oswalt, Wendell H. *The Kuskokwim River Drainage, Alaska: An Annotated Bibliography.* [College, Alaska, University of Alaska, 1965]. 73p. (Anthropological Papers of the University of Alaska, v. 13, no. 1).

Specialized bibliography of 483 items. Chiefly anthropological, but includes material on history and natural resources. The author points out the limitations on material from the Russian period and from newspapers, but his work offers access to much unfamiliar material.

Van Stone, James W. An annotated ethnohistorical bibliography of the Nushagak River Region, Alaska. *Fieldiana: Anthropology,* v. 54, no. 2; 1968: p. 149-189.

A specialized bibliography of 226 items. Prepared to indicate the value of the material for the anthropologists working in the area, and especially for the student of cultural change. The introduction covers archive collections and indicates the major sources used.

Wickersham, James. *A Bibliography of Alaskan Literature, 1724-1924.* Cordova, Alaska, Cordova Daily Times Print, 1927. 635p. (Miscellaneous Publications of the Alaska Agricultural College and School of Mines, v. 1, no. 1).

. . . containing the titles of all histories, travels, voyages, newspapers, periodicals, public documents, etc., printed in English, Russian, German, French, Spanish, etc., relating to, descriptive of, or published in Russian America or Alaska from 1724 to and including 1924. The first and classic bibliography on Alaska. 10,380 entries in two sections: 1, General Publications, arranged alphabetically under subjects; 2, United States Public Documents, arranged under departments, with general index.

SEE ALSO the general and specialized bibliographies in: Collins, *Eskimo Cultures,* 1961; Covarrubias, *The Eagle, the Jaguar and the Serpent,* 1954; Graburn and Strong, *Circumpolar Peoples,* 1973; Oswalt, *Alaskan Eskimos,* 1967; Ray, *Artists of the Tundra and the Sea,* 1961; Ray, *Eskimo Masks,* 1967; Ray, *The Eskimos of Bering Strait,* 1975; Swinton, *Sculpture of the Eskimo,* 1972.

Adney, Edwin T. and Chapelle, Howard I. *The Bark Canoes and Skin Boats of North America.* Washington, D. C., Smithsonian Institution, 1964. 242p. illus., bibl. (Bulletin of the U. S. National Museum, 230).

Based on Adney's notes and papers in The Mariner's Museum, Newport News, Virginia, edited and augmented by Chapelle. Chapter 7, Arctic Skin Boats, by Chapelle, p. 174-211, covers in detail the umiak and kayak with construction drawings and photographs.

Alaska. Dept. of Natural Resources. Division of Parks. *The Alaska Historic Preservation Act.* [Juneau, Alaska] 1975. 24p.

Presents the text from Chapter 35 of *Laws and Regulations Relating to Archaeology and Historic Preservation in Alaska.*

Alaska. University. *Anthropological Papers,* v. 1-, 1952-. College, Alaska, 1952-. illus.

An irregular serial. Major series of reports by scholars on archaeological and ethnological work in Alaska.

The Alaska Journal; History and Arts of the North. v. 1-, 1971-. Juneau, Alaska, Alaska Northwest Publishing Co., 1971-. illus.

Published quarterly. A semi-popular publication, usually well illustrated, offering good coverage of Native art and artists. Includes book reviews.

Anchorage, Alaska. The Anchorage Historical and Fine Arts Museum. *An Introduction to the Native Art of Alaska.* Anchorage, Alaska, Department of Parks and Recreations, 1972. 84p. illus., map, bibl.

Published in place of the usual exhibition catalog for the Alaska Festival of Native Arts, 1972. Covers prehistoric, historic and modern Eskimo and Indian art; arranged by material with illustrations chiefly from the museum's collections. Introduction by R. L. Shalkop, p. 2-9, gives a brief history. Alaskan Eskimo Carving and Engraving in Perspective, by Saradell Ard Frederick, p. 17-19.

Anchorage, Alaska. Anchorage Historical and Fine Arts Museum. *9th Alaska Festival of Native Arts,* June 2-30, 1974. [Anchorage, Alaska, 1974]. [16]p. illus.

Catalog of the art exhibition at the festival held each spring at the museum, as part of the Alaska Festival of Music, to promote the preservation, recognition and future development of Native Alaskan art forms. Gives illustrations and brief descriptions of the work shown.

Anchorage, Alaska. Anchorage Historical and Fine Arts Museum. *Peter Seeganna, an Artist; Retrospective Exhibition,* January 9 — February 3, 1975. [Anchorage, Alaska, 1975]. 20p. illus.

Catalog lists 33 works with 5 illustrations and a photograph of the artist; includes a brief discussion of his life and work by Joseph E. Senungetuk.

Anchorage, Alaska. Anchorage Historical and Fine Arts Museum. *St. Lawrence Island.* [Anchorage, Alaska, 1974]. [22]p. illus., map, bibl.

Catalog consists chiefly of illustrations of Okvik, Old Bering Sea and Punuk material together with examples of current Native work. Introduction by Mary Pat Wyatt, Curator of Collections.

Anderson, Douglas D. *Akmak; an Early Archaeological Assemblage from Onion Portage, Northwest Alaska.* Kobenhavn, Munksgaard, 1970. 70p. illus., maps, bibl. (Acta Arctica, 16).

Report on the 1966 excavation on the bank of the Kobuk River where the earliest remains of early sea mammal hunters north of the Aleutian Islands were found. The finds and their relationships to Asia are discussed.

Anderson, Douglas D. A Stone Age campsite at the gateway to America. *Scientific American,* v. 218, no. 6; 1968: p 24-33. illus., bibl.

Subtitle: Onion Portage in Alaska is an unusual site. It provides a record of human habitation going back at least 8,500 years, when its occupants were not far removed from their forebears in Asia. A preliminary popular article covering material in His *Akmak* above.

Anderson, H. D. and Eels, W. C. *Alaska Natives.* Stanford, Calif., Stanford University Press, 1935. 472p. illus., maps, bibl.

Report of a nine months survey made in 1930 "... of their sociological and educational status ... made under the auspices of the School of Education of Stanford University, at the request of the United States Office of Education ..." Offers recommendations for improvement in native education to maintain some of the old values in a changing situation.

Arctic Anthropology, v. 1-, 1962-. [Madison, Wis.] University of Wisconsin Press, 1962-. illus.

Published irregularly. ... an international journal devoted to all aspects of the science of man in the arctic, subarctic and contiguous regions of the world both past and present. A major journal, with emphasis on archaeology, reporting current research by specialists in the field.

Arnold, Robert D., Archibald, Janet [and others]. *Alaska Native Land Claims.* With a foreword by Emil Notti. [Anchorage, Alaska] The Alaska Native Foundation [1976]. 348p. illus., maps.

Divided into two parts: the first part, a series of historical sketches on Native peoples; the second part, articles on the Native Claims Act and its implementation now, with consideration of the effect on the future. Reprints the entire *Alaska Native Claims Settlement Act,* Public Law 92-203, 92nd Congress, H. R. 10367, December 18, 1971, with a guide to the sections, p. 300-329.

Appendices: A. The Alaska Native Claims Settlement Act; B. Village Corporations Eligible for Money and Land Benefits; C. Village Corporations Which Choose Former Reserves; D. Local Corporations, Four Named Cities; E. Local Corporations Certified As Groups; F. Village Corporations Appealing in Eligibility; G. Incorporators of the Twelve Regional Corporations; H. Alaska Federation of Natives.

A teacher's manual and student work book by Lydia Hays are published separately.

The Arts in Alaska; the Newsletter of the Alaska State Council on the Arts, 1973-. Anchorage, Alaska, The Alaska State Council on the Arts, 1973-. illus.

Published 5 times a year. Covers the arts in the State with some emphasis on Native arts and the projects supported by the Council.

Artscanada. *The Eskimo World.* Dec. 1971/Jan. 1972. no. 162/163. 146p. illus. (part col.), bibl.

Special issue: *The Eskimo World.* Appeared at the time of the Ottawa exhibition, *Sculpture/Inuit.* Chiefly Canadian material with some reference to Alaskan prehistoric and contemporary cultures. Good illustration of old and modern material, much of it in color. Contemporary Arts in Non-Western Societies, by Jacqueline Delange Fry, p. 96-101, offers an interesting discussion of the similarities and differences of the primitive arts.

Bandi, Hans G. *Eskimo Prehistory;* translated by Ann E. Keep. London, Methuen, 1969. 226p. illus., maps, bibl.

First published in German, 1965. A major general summary of Eskimo archaeology with good illustrations and an extensive bibliography. Milestones in Research, p. 35-46. Alaska, p. 47-130.

The Beaver Magazine of the North. *Eskimo Art,* Autumn, 1967. Winnipeg, Hudson's Bay Co., 1968. 98p. illus. (part col.), bibl.

Special issue: *Eskimo Art.* Chiefly Canadian material with good illustrations of old and contemporary art. Alaskan Eskimo Arts and Crafts, by Dorothy Jean Ray, p. 80-91, offers a general summary of Alaskan art with illustrations of major pieces.

Belcher, Edward. On the manufacture of works of art by the Esquimaux. *Transactions of the Ethnological Society of London,* 1; 1861: p. 129-146.

Interesting for the early date of a discussion of Eskimo art. The author was aboard the ship *Blossom* from 1825 to 1829 hoping to meet the Franklin expedition. Here he reports on objects he collected and the observations he made, chiefly at Cape Lisburne, with descriptions of houses, stone and jade tools, needlecases and personal ornaments.

Birket-Smith, Kaj. The Chugach Eskimo. *Nationalmuseets Skrifter, Etnografisk Raekke,* (Copenhagen) 6; 1953: p. 1-270. illus., map, bibl.

A standard ethnographic description based on information gathered with Frederica de Laguna on the first Danish-American Alaska Expedition of 1933. Offers description and illustration of the material culture with special reference to hunting equipment and basketry.

Birket-Smith, Kaj. Early collections from the Pacific Eskimo. *Nationalmuseets Skrifter, Etnografisk Raekke,* (Copenhagen) 1; 1941: p. [121]-163. illus., bibl.

Describes and illustrates the material in the Danish National Museum collected by Henrick Johan Holmberg in 1851. The material, mostly from Kodiak Island and the nearby mainland, includes tools, weapons and decorated skins and clothing.

Birket-Smith, Kaj. *Eskimos.* New York, Crown [1971]. 277p. illus. (part col.), bibl.

First published in Danish, 1935. Long the classic text on the Eskimo, with understandable emphasis on Greenland, but offering material on Alaska as well. This English edition offers the most colored illustrations, and adds The Hour of Crisis, by Diamond Jenness, p. 237-259. Jenness finds the Alaskan Eskimo making the best adjustment to the modern world of any of the Eskimo groups.

Boas, Franz. Decorative designs of Alaskan needlecases: a study in the history of conventional designs, based on materials in the U. S. National Museum. *Proceedings of the U. S. National Museum,* 34; 1908: p. 321-344. illus., bibl.

One of a series of studies of Native American symbolism and design. Covers designs from the area between the Yukon and Norton Sound. 8 plates of illustrations.

Burch, Ernest S. *Eskimo Kinsmen; Changing Family Relationships in Northwest Alaska.* St. Paul, Minn., West Publishing Co. 1975. 352p. bibl. (American Ethnological Society Monograph, 59).

A study of traditional kinship in the nineteenth century with a discussion of the change that has taken place since then.

Burland, Cottie A. *Eskimo Art.* London, Hamlyn, 1973. 96p. illus. (part col.), map, bibl.

A popular general survey useful for the good illustrations. Alaskan material from the British Museum is included.

Burr, Christina. *Eskimo Ivory Carvings in the Rochester Museum.* [Rochester, N. Y., Rochester Museum and Science Center] 1972. 88p. illus., bibl.

Describes the carvings in the collection with brief text, and illustrates the material with line drawings. The objects are mostly Alaskan, chiefly from Kodiak Island.

Cammann, Schuyler. Carvings in walrus ivory. *The University [of Pennsylvania] Museum Bulletin,* v. 18, no. 3; 1954: p. 3-31. illus., bibl.

A general article stressing technique. Ten illustrations of Eskimo and Northwest Coast Indian objects in the University Museum, Philadelphia. Short bibliography on walrus ivory.

Campbell, John M. *Archeological Studies Along the Proposed Trans-Alaska Oil Pipeline Route.* [Washington, D. C.] Arctic Institute of North America, 1973. 24p. illus., bibl. (Arctic Institute of North America Technical Paper, 26).

Describes and evaluates the work of a committee of anthropologists "formed to advise the Bureau of Land Management, U. S. Department of the Interior, on matters pertaining to archeological finds along the proposed route of the Alyeska Pipeline Service from Prudhoe Bay to Valdez, Alaska." Observations on the data from over 200 sites surveyed are assessed as offering an opportunity for study of material and areas not otherwise known.

Campbell, John M. *Prehistoric Relations Between the Arctic and Temperate Zones of North America,* ed. by John M. Campbell. Montreal, Arctic Institute of North America, 1962. 181p. illus., bibl. (Arctic Institute of North America Technical Paper, 11).

Papers from a symposium at the 25th Annual Meeting of the Society for American Archaeology. Reviews recent finds to date and then explores the relationships between the Arctic and areas to the south in papers offered by specialists in these areas.

Chance, Norman A. Culture change and integration; an Eskimo example. *American Anthropologist,* v. 62; 1960: p. 1028-1044. bibl.

Report of a study to test the theory that societies undergoing rapid change will be characterized by social disruption, made in 1958 at Kaktovik, a village near a radar station. Chance found the village able to adjust to change because of values within the culture.

Chance, Norman A. *The Eskimo of North Alaska.* New York, Holt, Rinehart and Winston [1966]. 107p. illus., map, bibl. (Case Studies in Cultural Anthropology).

General description of the traditional and contemporary life of the Natives living along the north coast of Alaska. Social structure and the belief system are stressed and considered to be as important for the Eskimo as the material aspects of life.

Chicago, Ill. Field Museum of Natural History. Eskimo masks: the world of Tareumiut. *Field Museum of Natural History Bulletin,* v. 40, no. 12; 1969: p. 2-4. illus.

Illustrates 14 masks from the temporary exhibition of the same title from November 29, 1969 through March 1, 1970. The masks, from the museum's collection, were collected in 1897 and 1927 by Miner W. Bruce and John Borden. For a more complete study see: Van Stone, *Masks of the Point Hope Eskimo*, 1968/1969.

Collaer, Paul. *Music of the Americas; an Illustrated Music Ethnology of the Eskimo and American Indian Peoples.* With contributions by Willard Rhodes [and others]. New York, Praeger [1973]. 207p. illus., bibl.

Translation from the German edition of 1967. A basic work including musical type, transcriptions and illustrations of musical instruments.

College, Alaska. University of Alaska Museum. *Eskimo Dolls in the Collection of the University of Alaska Museum.* [College, Alaska, 1973]. 4p. and poster.

Text by Dinah W. Larsen. Brief introduction and poster illustrating 36 dolls from various areas and archaeological sites. Makers' names are given for contemporary dolls.

Collins, Henry B. *Archaeology of St. Lawrence Island, Alaska.* Washington, D. C., The Smithsonian Institution, 1937. 431p. illus., map, plans, bibl. (Smithsonian Miscellaneous Collections, v. 96, no. 1).

The major work on St. Lawrence Island based on the Smithsonian excavations of 1930-1931. Offers discussion and illustration of Old Bering Sea and Punuk material, with discussion of the relationship to other areas, especially Siberia.

Collins, Henry B. Composite masks: Chinese and Eskimo. *Anthropologia,* v. 13; 1971: p. 271-278. illus., bibl.

Compares Ipiutak masks with Shang marble masks from China, and discusses possible influences and relationships.

Collins, Henry B. Eskimo cultures. In *Encyclopedia of World Art,* v. 5. New York, McGraw-Hill, 1961. col. 1-28. illus., bibl.

One of the most complete short summary articles offering a thorough introduction to the subject, with emphasis on the art. Major pieces are illustrated (plates 1-12), and an extensive bibliography is appended.

Collins, Henry B. The Okvik Figurine; Madonna or Bear Mother? *Folk, Dansk Etnografisk Tidsskrift,* v. 11-12; 1969/70: p. 125-132. illus., bibl.

Part of a special issue of essays presented to Erik Holtved, the Danish Eskimo scholar. Other papers on the Bear Cult and the Animal Cult in Asia and America are included. Collins suggests the Okvik Madonna and other such figures may represent the Bear Mother of legend.

Collins, Henry B. The origin and antiquity of the Eskimo. *Annual Report of the Smithsonian Institution,* 1950; 1951: p. 423-467. illus., bibl.

Summarizes various theories, and concludes that the early maritime culture from which Eskimo culture developed was derived from the late neolithic cultures of central Asia.

Collins, Henry B. *Outline of Eskimo Prehistory.* Washington, D. C., Smithsonian Institution, 1940. 59p. maps, bibl. (Smithsonian Miscellaneous Collections, v. 100).

Offers a brief review of modern Eskimo culture and an outline of archaeological work to date with a discussion of the origin of Eskimo culture.

Collins, Henry B. *Prehistoric Art of the Alaskan Eskimo.* Washington, D. C., The Smithsonian Institution, 1929. 52p. illus. (Smithsonian Miscellaneous Collections, v. 81, no. 14).

Stress is on ivory materials from St. Lawrence Island and the Punuk Islands, and their relationships to other areas.

Copenhagen. Nationalmuseet. *Arctic Peoples and American Indians.* Copenhagen, 1941. 112p. illus. (Guides to the National Museum).

Covers the material in the collection, including material from the Fifth Thule Expedition of 1921-24, and the Danish-American Alaska Expedition of 1939 and 1949-50.

Covarrubias, Miguel. *The Eagle, the Jaguar and the Serpent; Indian Art of the Americas: North America: Alaska, Canada, the United States.* New York, Knopf, 1954. 314p. illus. (part col.), maps, bibl.

A major work on the subject of North American Native art. The Arctic, p. 137-163, offers one of the best general introductions to the art of the Eskimo, heavily supported with illustration

and an extensive bibliography. Bibliography, p. 297-314.

Dall, William H. Masks, labrets and certain aboriginal customs, with an inquiry into the bearing of their geographical distribution. *U. S. Bureau of American Ethnology Annual Report,* v. 3; 1884: p. 67-203. illus., bibl.

Mostly a discussion of masks from the Americas with some emphasis on Alaska. Describes and illustrates masks from Kodiak Island, the Kuskokwim River area, Norton Sound, the Bering Strait area and Point Barrow.

Davidson, Art. *Eskimo Hunting of Bowhead Whales.* Anchorage, Alaska, Rural Alaska Community Action Program, in cooperation with Community Enterprise Development Corporation and the John Muir Institute for Environmental Studies [197-]. 37p. illus., map.

Offers "... a review of existing information on the relation of Eskimos and Bowhead whales in the 1970's." Covers the problem of extinction of the whale, present regulations and the importance of the whale in Eskimo life, offering possible suggestions for the future. Whaling and the crafts from bone and baleen are illustrated.

Davidson, Carla. Arctic twilight: the paintings of Kivetoruk Moses. *American Heritage,* v. 26, no. 4; 1975: p. 16-21. illus. (1 col.).

Brief text on the artist, who now lives in Nome, with illustration of nine of his paintings and a photograph of Moses and his wife.

Dockstader, Frederick J. *Indian Art in America; the Arts and Crafts of the North American Indian.* Greenwich, Conn., New York Graphic Society [1961]. 224p. illus. (part col.), map, bibl.

Republished in 1968 as *Indian Art in North America; Arts and Crafts,* with additions to the bibliography. A short discussion of Eskimo art in a general North American context. Important for the good color illustrations, mostly from the major collection of The Museum of the American Indian, Heye Foundation, New York.

Douglas, Frederic and Harnoncourt, René d'. *Indian Art of the United States.* New York, The Museum of Modern Art [1941]. 219p. illus. (part col.), maps, bibl.

Catalog of a major early exhibition that did much to popularize Native American art. The Engravers of the Arctic, p. 41-42. The Eskimo Hunters of the Arctic, p. 169-180. Illustrations of major pieces from various collections.

Durham, Floyd E. *Ancient and Current Methods of Taking the Bowhead Whale.* Anchorage, Alaska, University of Alaska, 1974. 15p. illus., bibl.

The aboriginal method of taking whale by harpoon is described and the change to the use of the whale bomb and its almost exclusive use today is discussed. As the use of bombs wastes the whales, a return to the old method is suggested as a means of conservation. Old and new tools are illustrated.

Eluard, Paul. La nuit est à une dimension. *Cahiers d'Art,* 10e année, no. 5-6; 1935: p. 99-101, 113. illus.

Subtitle: Exposition de masques et objets esquimaux et masques et objets de l'Amérique de N. O. de la collection Charles Raton. Offers especially fine illustrations of masks in a major French collection.

Emmons, George T. *Jade in British Columbia and Alaska, and Its Use by the Natives.* New York, Museum of the American Indian, Heye Foundation, 1923. 53p. Illus. (part col.), bibl. (Indian Notes and Monographs [Miscellaneous Series], 35).

Discussion of the use of jade (nephrite) as ornament and tool by the Indian and the Eskimo. Describes and illustrates the Eskimo man's labret and various cutting tools using jade for the blade.

Encyclopedia of Indians of the Americas. [Keith Irvine, general ed.]. v. 1; 1974. St. Clair Shores, Mich., Scholarly Press, 1974-. illus. (19 v. in preparation).

A projected 20 volume work on the Natives of North and South America which will include the Eskimo. Volume one, Conspectus/Chronology, offers a description of the Encyclopedia along with general articles and a chronology from 25,000 B. C. to 1974. Later volumes will be a series of articles written by various specialists and arranged in alphabetical order.

Erkin, Annette E. *Modern Alaskan Native Material Culture.* College, Alaska, University of Alaska Museum, 1972. 16p.

A brief description of the Native peoples of Alaska intended to be complementary and supplementary to the exhibit, *Contract and Change,* produced by the Modern Alaska Native Material Culture Project.

SEE ALSO Oswalt, *Modern Alaskan Native Material Culture.*

Fagg, William B. *Eskimo Art in the British Museum.* [London] The British Museum [1972]. 48p. illus., map.

Description and illustration of material in the collections which includes Alaskan material, notably masks collected by Kotzebue.

Flack, Evaline. Les Masques eskimo et aléoutes de la collection Pinart. [par] Evaline Lot-Flack. *Journal de la Société des Américanistes,* n. s. T. 46; 1957: p. [5]-43. illus., bibl.

Describes and illustrates 82 masks (72 Eskimo) collected by Alphonse Pinart 1870-1872 from southwest Alaska and Kodiak Island. 10 plates of illustration.

Flack, Roger and Flack, Evaline. *Catalogue analytique et descriptif des têtes de harpons eskimo du Musée de l'Homme.* [Paris] Musée de l'Homme, 1963. 52p. illus., bibl. (Catalogues du Musée de l'Homme, sér. G, Arctiques, 1).

A thorough and complete study of harpoon heads in the collection of the Musée de l'Homme with a suggested typology. Most of the material is Dorset, but "Punuk-Birnirk" material is also included.

Ford, James A. *Eskimo Prehistory in the Vicinity of Point Barrow, Alaska.* New York, American Museum of Natural History, 1959. 272p. illus., maps, bibl. (Anthropological Papers of the American Museum of Natural History, v. 47, pt. 1).

Based on work done in 1931-32 and 1956 at several sites. Discusses the material found and concludes that the Birnirk stage evolved from Okvik and Old Bering Sea.

Frost, O. W. *Cross-cultural Arts in Alaska,* ed. by O. W. Frost. Anchorage, Alaska, Alaska Methodist University Press, 1970. 96p. illus. (Alaska Review, v. 4, no. 2).

Special issue: *Cross-cultural Arts in Alaska.* Includes Indian and Eskimo arts with some emphasis on the traditional arts, but also including the work of contemporary artists now adapting the traditional forms to their work. Material on the Arts Council and government support, by Mary Hale, p. 83-93. Heavily illustrated.

Giddings, James L. *Ancient Men of the Arctic.* New York, Knopf, 1967. 391p. illus., maps.

Published after the death of the author. The Introduction, by Henry B. Collins, summarizes and evaluates the work of Giddings. The book is a narrative account of Gidding's experience in Alaska, especially at Cape Denbigh and Onion Portage, as well as a general account of the archaeology of the area.

Giddings, James L. The archaeology of Bering Strait. *Current Anthropology,* v. 1; 1960: p. 121-138. map, bibl.

A landmark review article giving the current status of the archaeology to date, with the author's interpretations, and offering a chronology chart. Comments by: Chester S. Chard, Henry B. Collins, David M. Hopkins, Frederica de Laguna, Helge Larsen, and M. G. Levin. Collins gives a long comment, p. 131-137, disagreeing with the author as to the relationship of the Bering Sea cultures.

Giddings, James L. *The Archaeology of Cape Denbigh.* Providence, R. I., Brown University Press, 1964. 331p. illus., bibl.

Report of a four year study made 1948-1952 on the Denbigh Flint Complex at Norton Sound. Dates of 4-5,000 years old are given, and relationships to the European Mesolithic and Palaeolithic, as well as to Woodland North America, are suggested.

Giffen, Naomi M. *The Rôle of Men and Women in Eskimo Culture.* Chicago, Ill., The University of Chicago, 1930. 113p. bibl. (The University of Chicago Publications in Anthropology, Ethnological Series).

A brief, somewhat popular text drawn from the literature. Mostly valuable today for the extensive bibliography which covers the older literature.

Giraux, Louis. Gravures coloriées sur dents de morse des Esquimaux de l'Alaska. *Journal de la Société des Américanistes de Paris,* n. s. T. 18; 1926: p. 91-102. illus., bibl.

After a brief description of the engraving technique, the author identifies the animals depicted on two examples from the nineteenth century.

Graburn, Nelson H. H. and Strong, B. Stephen. *Circumpolar Peoples: an Anthropological Perspective*. Pacific Palisades, Calif., Goodyear Publishing Co. [1973]. 236p. illus., maps, bibl. (Goodyear Regional Anthropology Series).

A thorough introductory guide to the northern peoples, with valuable bibliographical essays on the Eskimos, p. 171-177, and Alaska, p. 209-212. Includes a guide to journals and films.

Gubser, Nicholas J. *The Nunamiut Eskimo; Hunters of the Caribou*. New Haven, Conn., Yale University Press, 1965. 384p. maps, bibl.

A contemporary description of the life of a group of 100 North Alaskan Eskimo living in the Anaktuvuk Pass, based on work there in 1959 and 1960. Only limited carving in ivory is done there now.

Haberland, Wolfgang. *The Art of North America*. New York, Crown [1964]. 251p. illus. (part col.), bibl. (Art of the World Series).

Translated from the German by Wayne Dynes. Chapter III, The North, p. 25-46, offers an especially good short survey of Eskimo art, with some emphasis on prehistoric Alaska. Good illustrations, chiefly from European collections.

Haselberger, Herta. Method of studying ethnological art. *Current Anthropology*, v. 2; 1961: p. 341-348. bibl.

A landmark article in the field of primitive art. Offers a history of the field, and discusses the need for investigation of material, technique, purpose, content and form. The study of the artist and the society is stressed. Comments are included from specialists in various areas. Edmund Carpenter comments on the Eskimo, p. 361-362.

Carpenter's comment reprinted as The Eskimo Artist In *Anthropology and Art* [ed. by] Charlotte M. Otten, Garden City, N. Y., The Natural History Press, 1971, p. [163]-171.

Hawkes, Ernest W. *The Dance Festivals of the Alaskan Eskimo*. Philadelphia, Pa., University Museum, 1914. 41p. illus. (University [of Pennsylvania] Museum Anthropological Publications, v. 6, no. 2).

Description of dance festivals and dance houses in the Bering Strait district at St. Michael and on the Diomede Islands. Includes illustrations of house

plans and of the dances.

Hawkes, Ernest W. *The "Inviting-In" Feast of the Alaskan Eskimo*. Ottawa, Govn't. Print. Bureau, 1913. 20p. illus. (Canada. Geological Survey, Memoir, v. 45, no. 3; Anthropological Series, 3).

A description of feast at St. Michael in 1912. Describes and discusses the dance house, the dances and the music. Suggests that the festival is an appeal for future success in hunting. 13 plates illustrate masks, drums and asking-sticks.

Himmelheber, Hans. *Eskimokünstler; Ergebnisse einer Reise in Alaska*. [2. Aufl.]. Eisenach, E. Röth [1953]. 136p. illus., map, bibl. (Bücher der Brücke).

First edition, 1938, with title: *Teilergebnis einer ethnographischen Expedition in Alaska von Juni 1936 bis April 1937*. Second edition is expanded with more illustration. Report of a trip along the whole coast of Alaska with description and illustration of artists, masks, drawings and ivory carvings. 44 plates of illustration.

Hipszer, Hermine. Les Masques de chamans du Musée Ethnographiques de Berlin. *Baessler-Archiv*, N. F., Bd. 19, no. 2; 1971: p. 421-450. illus.

Description of masks collected by John Adrian Jacobson with II illustrations. New attributions to southwestern Alaska and Kodiak Island are given by comparison with pieces in other collections.

Hodge, Frederick W. *Handbook of American Indians North of Mexico*, ed. by Frederick Webb Hodge. Washington, D. C., Government Printing Office, 1907-1910. 2v. illus., map. (U. S. Bureau of American Ethnology Bulletin, 30).

Long the standard reference on the subject despite the early date; arranged alphabetically by short topic. Includes the Eskimo. Soon to be superseded by Sturtevant, *Handbook of North American Indians*, 1976? (In preparation).

Hoffman, Walter J. The graphic art of the Eskimos, based on the collections in the National Museum. *Report of the U. S. National Museum*, 1895; 1897: p. 739-968. illus., bibl.

The classic early work on the subject, with especial reference to engraving on ivories from Alaska. 82 plates of illustration. Specimens Referred to in Present Paper, p. 958-968, constitutes a virtual catalog of the material in the

museum at the time. Appendix: Gesture Signs of Eskimos, p. 948-958.

Houston, Tex. Museum of Fine Arts. *The Eskimo*. Sponsored by Humble Oil & Refining Co., September 20 to November 23, 1969. Houston, Tex. [1969]. 29p. illus., map.

Short introduction by Mary Hancock Buxton. Catalog illustrates and describes 61 pieces, chiefly from Alaska, borrowed from private and institutional collections.

Hrdlicka, Ales. Anthropological survey in Alaska. *U. S. Bureau of American Ethnology Annual Report*, v. 46; 1930: p. 19-374. illus., maps.

Observations made in 1926 by the well-known physical anthropologist. Includes fine illustrations of carved patterns and wooden dolls.

Hughes, Charles C. *An Eskimo Village in the Modern World*, with the collaboration of Jane M. Hughes. Ithaca, N. Y., Cornell University Press [1960]. 419p. illus., maps, bibl. (Cornell Studies in Anthropology).

A study made in 1954 and 1955 of the St. Lawrence Island village of Gamble (Sivokak) where changes from traditional to modern living have been caused by seasonal work and a money economy resulting in a movement to the mainland. Hughes offers suggestions to integrate the old and the new ways of life.

Hultkrantz, Åke. Die Religion der amerikanischen Arktis. In *Die Religionen Nordeurasiens und der amerikanischen Arktis*, von Ivar Paulson, Åke Hultkrantz [und] Karl Jettmar, Stuttgart, W. Kohlhammer [1962], Die Religionen der Menscheit, 3, p. 357-415. bibl.

A description of Eskimo religion in general with some reference to Alaska. Covers gods, spirits, hunting rites and ceremonies, with especial reference to shamanism and the importance of animals.

Institute of Alaskan Native Arts Committee. *Report of the Institute of Alaskan Native Arts Committee on a Study of the Proposed Development of an Educational Institution for: Native Cultures in the State of Alaska*. Fairbanks, Alaska, 1975. 31p. illus.

Illustrated by Native crafts and art works. Report compiled by Laura Bergt, Mary Jane Fate and Thomas Richards, Jr. Brief reports on the present teaching facilities in the state and description of the survey of artists for their opinions on a proposed Institute of Alaskan Native Arts under the Indian Arts and Crafts Board along the lines of the Institute of American Indian Arts in Santa Fe, New Mexico.

Israel, Heinz. Alaskische Spielbretter aus Walrosszähnen. *Abhandlungen und Berichte des Staatlichen Museums für Völkerkunde, Dresden,* Bd. 22; 1963: p. [15]-[24]. illus., bibl.

Descriptions and illustrations of examples from museums in Paris and Frankfurt, and a private collection in Zurich.

Israel, Heinz. Beinschnitzerie der Eskimo. *Abhandlungen und Berichte des Staatlichen Museums für Völkerkunde, Dresden,* Bd. 33; 1971: p. [113]-139. illus., bibl.

Description and illustration of pieces in the Herrenhuter Collection of the Oberlausitz Museum für Völkerkunde. 47 illustrations. The pieces were collected by Herrenhuter in the 1880's while he was a missionary in Alaska.

Jenness, Diamond. *Eskimo Administration: I. Alaska.* Montreal, Arctic Institute of North America, 1962. 64p. map, bibl. (Arctic Institute of North America Technical Paper, 10).

One of a 5 volume study of Eskimo administration published by the Arctic Institute of North America. Reviews the Eskimo under government jurisdiction by three periods significant in terms of policy: 1867-1896; 1896-1939; and 1939-1960.

Jenness, Diamond. The Eskimos of northern Alaska: a study in the effect of civilization. *Geographical Review,* v. 5; 1918: p. 89-101. illus., map.

Interesting chiefly for the early date of the study. Describes the change from hunting to trapping, and the resulting effect of economic change on the Eskimo.

Josephson, Karla. *Alaska and the Law of the Sea; Use of the Sea by Alaska Natives — a Historical Perspective.* Anchorage, Alaska, Arctic Environmental Information and Data Center, University of Alaska, 1974. 95p. illus., map, bibl.

Describes and illustrates traditional hunting and fishing methods for all of the Native peoples of Alaska. Methods and tools are described by area, and the dependence of the people on the sea is stressed.

Keim, Gay. *Alaskan Ornamentation;* illus.

by Jean English. [College, Alaska] University of Alaska Museum, 1972. 16p. illus.

Published as a part of the Alaska Native Material Culture Project. Describes and illustrates the jewelry, ornamentation and tattooing of the Eskimos and Indians.

Keithahn, Edward L. *Native Alaskan Art in the State Historical Museum, Juneau, Alaska.* Juneau, Alaska, Historical Library and Museum, 1959. 20p. illus.

Photos and text by Edward L. Keithahn. A brief introduction covers the art and the artist; chiefly illustration of prehistoric, historic and modern pieces in the collection. 33 plates.

Laguna, Frederica de. *Chugash Prehistory; the Archaeology of Prince William Sound, Alaska.* Seattle, Wash., University of Washington Press, 1956. 289p. illus., maps, bibl. (University of Washington Publications in Anthropology, 13).

Based on work in the area with Birket-Smith in 1930 and 1933. Offers a study of the artifacts and pictographs, and attempts to reconstruct the prehistoric life of the area.

Laguna, Frederica de. A comparison of Eskimo and Palaeolithic art. *American Journal of Archaeology,* s. 2, v. 36; 1936: p. 477-511; v. 37; 1937: p. 77-107. illus., bibl.

A monumental study concluding that Eskimo art is not a survival of, or directly related to the art of the European Palaeolithic. Although made before the discovery of the Ipiutak and Okvik materials, many find her conclusions still valid. For other views see the works of Collins.

Laguna, Frederica de. Peintures rupestres eskimo. *Journal de la Société des Américanistes,* n.s. 25; 1933: p. 17-30. illus., bibl.

Illustrates and describes rock drawings in the area of Cook Inlet and Kachemak Bay with reference to local Indian material and possible relationship to the European Palaeolithic.

Lantis, Margaret. *Alaskan Eskimo Ceremonialism.* New York, J. J. Augustin [1947]. 127p. maps, bibl. (American Ethnological Society Monographs, 11).

The basic work on the subject covering the rituals, their distribution, and relationship to the culture as a whole. Some emphasis is given to shamanism.

Masks, dress, adornment, music and musical instruments are discussed.

Lantis, Margaret. The Alaskan Whale Cult and its affinities. *American Anthropologist,* v. 40; 1938: p. 438-464. bibl.

Describes the ritual of the Whale Cult in the north Pacific, Bering Sea area, and the Asiatic and American Arctic, finding a basic pattern throughout the area.

Lantis, Margaret. The Religion of the Eskimos. In *Forgotten Religions,* ed. by V. Ferm, New York, Philosophical Library, 1950, p. 311-319. bibl.

The basic statement on the subject. Covers shamanism, cosmology, society and religion, and the various spirits and dieties. Finding a uniformity with local differences, the author concludes that the religion mitigated physical threats and unified the community.

Lantis, Margaret. The Social culture of the Nunivak Eskimo. *Transactions of the American Philosophical Society,* n. s. 35; 1946: p. 156-323. illus., bibl.

The standard ethnographic study of this group of Bering Sea Eskimo based on work done in 1939 and 1940.

Larsen, Helge. Archaeological investigations in southwestern Alaska. *American Antiquity,* v. 15; 1950: p. 177-186. bibl.

One of the few studies of the area. "Our investigations thus seem to prove that the Neo-Eskimo Culture did not stop at Norton Sound . . . but spread as far as the Pacific. Finally, we learned the importance of pottery in Eskimo culture."

Larsen, Helge and Rainey, Froelich. *Ipiutak and the Arctic Whale Hunting Culture.* New York, The American Museum of Natural History, 1948. 276p. illus., bibl. (Anthropological Papers of the American Museum of Natural History, v. 42).

The full scientific report of the monumental finds at Point Hope in 1938-1941 of material 2000 years old, having resemblances to the Asiatic Animal Style. 101 plates.

McGhee, Robert. Differential artistic productivity in the Eskimo cultural tradition. *Current Anthropology,* v. 17; 1976: p. 203-220. bibl.

Discusses the apparent differences in quantity and quality of artistic materials produced during different periods of Eskimo culture in relation to certain cultural variables. Concludes that the art production does not appear to be correlated with any single variable in the social, economic or belief system of the culture. Comments from twelve specialists in the field are included along with a reply by McGhee.

Mason, J. Alden. Eskimo pictorial art. *The [University] Museum Journal*, v. 18; 1927: p. 248-283. illus.

Describes and illustrates 16 examples of engraved implements, bow drills and boxes in the collection of the University Museum, Philadelphia.

Mason, Otis T. Aboriginal American basketry: studies in a textile art without machinery. *U. S. National Museum Annual Report*, 1902; 1904: p. 171-548. illus. (part col.), maps, bibl.

The classic study of basketry with many illustrations from the collection of the U. S. National Museum. Eskimo Baskets, p. 395-403. Includes a list of U. S. collections, p. 541.

Mason, Otis T. Aboriginal American harpoons: a study in ethnic distribution and invention. *Report of the U. S. National Museum*, 1900; 1902: p. 189-304. illus., bibl.

A general survey for the Americas. Chapter VI, Arctic Harpoons, p. 236-303, includes material from arctic Alaska and Kodiak Island.

Mason, Otis T. Aboriginal skin dressing; a study based on material in the U .S. National Museum. *Report of the U. S. National Museum*, 1889; 1891: p. 553-589. illus., bibl.

Classic study of skins and skin dressing with some emphasis on Alaskan and other Eskimos. Discusses skins used, tools and methods of dressing. Heavily illustrated with material in the U. S. National Museum, including tools collected by E. W. Nelson.

Mason, Otis T. Primitive travel and transportation. *Report of the U. S. National Museum*, 1894; 1896: p. 237-593. illus., bibl.

Arranged by means of transport. Includes considerable Eskimo material with discussion of snow shoes and foot wear as well as sleds and equipment.

Miles, Charles. *Indian and Eskimo Artifacts of North America*, with a foreword by Frederick J. Dockstader. Chicago, Ill.,

H. Regnery Co., 1963. 244p. illus. (part col.), bibl.

Popular text including 1550 small reference photographs. Arranged by topic with an index by tribe, including Eskimo.

Miles, Charles and Bovis, Pierre. *American Indian and Eskimo Basketry; a Key to Identification*. San Francisco, Calif., P. Bovis [1969]. 144p. illus., map, bibl.

Popular work consisting chiefly of small illustrations with brief text. Arranged by method of construction as the key to identification.

Minneapolis, Minn. Walker Art Center. *American Indian Art; Form and Tradition*. An exhibition organized by Walker Art Center, Indian Art Association [and] The Minneapolis Institute of Arts, 22 October — 31 December 1972. [Minneapolis, Minn., The Walker Art Center and The Minneapolis Institute of Arts, 1972]. 154p. illus. (part col.), bibl.

A major recent exhibition with illustrations from important American collections. Eskimo Sculpture [by] Dorothy Jean Ray, p. 93-97. Catalog Of the Exhibition, p. 117-145.

Morgan, Lael. *And the Land Provides; Alaskan Natives in a Year of Transition*. Garden City, N. Y., Doubleday, 1974. 325p. map.

A journalist's account of the year she spent with the Natives just after the Land Claims Settlement of December, 1971. Attempts to "chronicle the transition of the Alaskan Natives from a subsistence to a money economy." Includes illustrations of present day life.

Murdock, John. Ethnological results of the Point Barrow Expedition. *U. S. Bureau of American Ethnology Annual Report*, 9; 1892: p. 1-441. illus., map, bibl.

A major source on art and life of the late nineteenth century Eskimo of the area. Report by the naturalist and observer with the U. S. Army on the International Polar Expedition to Point Barrow, Alaska. Records his observations of a two year stay and describes the material he collected. 428 illustrations of objects now in the U. S. National Museum.

Nelson, Edward W. The Eskimo about Bering Strait. *U. S. Bureau of American Ethnology Annual Report*, v. 18; 1899: p. 19-518. illus., bibl.

Important source for the late nine-

teenth century Eskimo. Based on the author's stay at St. Michael's fur trading station, 1877-1881. Describes his observations and the materials collected. 165 illustrations of objects now in the U.S. National Museum.

Nelson, Richard K. *Hunters of the Northern Ice*. Chicago, Ill., The University of Chicago Press [1969]. 429p. illus., maps, bibl.

First of a multidisciplinary investigation of Wainwright under the aegis of the International Biological Program. Complete and systematic study of hunting, done mostly at Wainwright in 1964 and 1966; illustrated with the author's photographs. Chapter 18, The Eskimo as Hunter, p. 373-382, stresses the importance of hunting for the Eskimo way of life.

Neuchâtel. Musée d'Ethnographie. *Les Esquimaux, hier . . . aujourd'hui*, du 4 juillet au 31 décembre 1976. [Neuchâtel, 1976]. 96p. illus., map, bibl.

Catalog of a major exhibition showing pieces from Canadian, Danish and Swiss museums, and including short articles by various specialists. Les Esquimaux d'aujourd'hui, par R. Petersen, p. 11-15. Contribution suisse à l'archéologie des Esquimaux, par H. G. Bandi, p. 19-25. Material collected in 1967 by Bandi at Gamble and St. Lawrence Island is included.

Oswalt, Wendell H. *Alaskan Eskimos*. San Francisco, Calif., Chandler Pub. Co.; distributors: Science Research Associates, Chicago [1967]. 297p. illus. (part col.), maps, bibl. (Chandler Publications in Anthropology and Sociology).

Perhaps the most complete single volume introduction. Covers all aspects of the people from prehistory to the present with documentation and discussion of various points of view. Cultural Origins, Prehistory and Recent Studies of Origins, p. 36-60, offers what amounts to a survey of the literature on Eskimo archaeology, as well as a complete discussion of the problem of Eskimo origins. Bibliography, p. 261-279.

Oswalt, Wendell H. *Modern Alaskan Native Material Culture*. College, Alaska, University of Alaska Museum, 1972. 130p. map, bibl.

"The Modern Alaskan Native Material Culture project was conceived in two phases. The first was to identify and collect objects and information that illustrate the continuity of traditional elements in native cultures and to document the changes which have occurred since historic contact, as illustrated by current technology." Includes Indian and Aleut. Collection Inventory, p. 97-130.

Phase 2 published as *Modern Alaskan Native Culture,* College, Alaska, University of Alaska Museum, 1973, 21p., illus., reports on the exhibition Contact and Change, at the museum, and on five smaller exhibitions throughout the state.

Oswalt, Wendell H. *Napaskiak; an Alaskan Eskimo Community.* Tucson, Ariz., The University of Arizona Press [1963]. 178p. illus., bibl.

Based on work done in 1955 and 1956 on the Kuskokwim River near Bethel. The experiences of a typical family moving into a money economy are described and analyzed.

Oswalt, Wendell H. A new collection of Old Bering Sea I artifacts. *Anthropological Papers of the University of Alaska,* v. 5, no. 2; 1957: p. 91-96. illus., bibl.

Report with discussion and illustration of a new find of figurines, harpoon heads, and tools carved in the style of the Old Bering Sea culture.

Oswalt, Wendell H. Traditional storyknife tales of Yuk girls. *Proceedings of the American Philosophical Society,* 108; 1964: p. 310-336. illus., bibl.

A study of stories and drawings made with storyknives at Napaskiak and an interpretation of them as a part of the child's world view. The storyknife is illustrated and described.

Phebus, George. *Alaskan Eskimo Life in the 1890's as Sketched by Native Artists.* Washington, D. C., Smithsonian Press, 1972. 168p. illus., maps, bibl.

Presents drawings and water colors made by various students in public and mission schools under the jurisdiction of the Bureau of Education of the Department of the Interior. The drawings are described, with reference to the literature of the time, and interpreted as to the activities portrayed. 120 illustrations.

Philadelphia, Pa. University Museum. *Arctic Art,* winter 1957-1958. Philadelphia, Pa., 1957. 16p. cover illus.

Check list of 294 (188 Alaskan) items shown at a major exhibition, with an introduction, Arctic Art, by Froelich Rainey.

Rainey, Froelich G. Discovering Alaska's oldest town. *National Geographic Magazine,* v. 82; 1942: p. 318-336. illus.

Subtitle: . . . a scientist finds ivory-eyed skeletons of a mysterious people and joins modern Eskimos in the dangerous spring whale hunt. Popular article on Point Hope and the Ipiutak culture with good illustrations.

Rainey, Froelich G. *Eskimo Prehistory: the Okvik Site on the Punuk Islands.* New York, The American Museum of Natural History, 1941. 117p. illus., bibl. (Anthropological Papers of the American Museum of Natural History, v. 37, pt. 4).

The full scientific report on the discoveries made on the Punuk Islands and St. Lawrence Island, with a discussion of the possible relationship of Okvik to other cultures.

Rainey, Froelich G. *The Ipiutak Culture: Excavations at Point Hope, Alaska.* [Reading, Mass., Addison-Wesley Publishing Co., 1971] 32p. illus., bibl.

A McCaleb Module in Anthropology from the series Addison-Wesley Modular Publications. A description of the author's excavations with Larsen in 1938-1941, and a discussion of their meaning in the light of later work. Interpretation, p. 23-27. Thirty Years Later, p. 27-32. Includes comparative charts on the status of Arctic cultural sequences ca. 1937, ca. 1948 and ca. 1970.

Rainey, Froelich G. *The Whale Hunters of Tigara.* New York, American Museum of Natural History, 1947. 53p. illus., bibl. (Anthropological Papers of the American Museum of Natural History, v. 41, pt. 2).

Report of a study made at Point Hope in 1940 which describes the life there and the changes made since contact with whites.

Rainey, Froelich G. and Ralph, Elizabeth. Radio carbon dating in the Arctic. *American Antiquity,* v. 24; 1959: p. 365-374. bibl.

Offers the first series for the Arctic from the laboratory of the University of Pennsylvania. A chronology of the culture periods used in Larsen and Rainey, *Ipiutak,* 1948, is given.

Rasmussen, Knud. *Across Arctic America; Narrative of the Fifth Thule Expedition.* New York, Putnam's, 1927. 388p. illus., maps.

First published in Danish, 1925. Narrative account of his sled journey from Greenland to Alaska for the Fifth Thule Expedition, 1921-24. A popular introduction to the Arctic and to the work of the expedition and its leader.

Rasmussen, Knud. *The Alaskan Eskimos, as Described in the Posthumous Notes of Dr. Knud Rasmussen,* by H. Ostermann, ed. after the latter's death with the assistance of E. Holtved. Copenhagen, Gyldendalske Boghandel, 1952. 291p. illus. (Reports of the Fifth Thule Expedition, 1921-24, v. 10, no. 3).

Contains the journal of his trip for the expedition, and ethnographic notes and folktales from northern Alaska, the Bering Strait, King Island, and Nome. Masks, ritual objects and hunting gear are described and illustrated. Especially strong on folklore.

Ray, Dorothy Jean. *Artists of the Tundra and the Sea.* Seattle, Wash., University of Washington Press, 1961. 170p. illus., bibl.

Major study of ivory carving and the carvers with 113 illustrations and a bibliography of sources. Covers prehistoric and modern carving with discussion of the material, technique and design. Nome and Happy Jack, p. 3-12. The Artist's Standards, p. 132-142. The Artist's Concept of Realism, p. 143-153. The Artist: Past and Future, p. 154-156. Appendix: Characteristic Motifs of Periods of Eskimo Carving, p. 157-161. Bibliography, p. 163-165.

Ray, Dorothy Jean. *Eskimo Masks; Art and Ceremony.* Photos. by Alfred A. Blaker. Seattle, Wash., University of Washington Press [1967]. 246p. illus. (part col.), bibl.

Study of masks in the Robert H. Lowie Museum of Anthropology, University of California, Berkeley. Illustration of the entire collection and pieces from other west coast museums on 82 plates. A thorough discussion and catalog of the west Alaskan masks based on the literature and field work, supported by references. Bibliography, p. 223-235, indicates illustration of masks, as well as information on collections at the end of the entries.

Ray, Dorothy Jean. *The Eskimos of Bering Strait, 1650-1898.* Seattle, Wash., University of Washington Press [1975]. 305p. illus., maps, bibl.

An in-depth study of the history of the area and the people, heavily documented with an extensive bibliography. Covers the early explorations of Bering, Cook, Kobelev and others, the Russian period, the search for Sir John Franklin and the Alaska Purchase. Chapter 17, The Eskimo and Domesticated Reindeer, p. 226-240. Chapter 13, Bering Strait Culture, 1833-67, p. 170-184. Chapter 18, Bering Strait Culture, 1867-98, p. 241-253. Chapter 15, Artifacts, Whaling and Mining, p. 195-204. References Used, p. 259-282.

Ray, Dorothy Jean. *Graphic arts of the Alaskan Eskimo.* [Washington, D. C.] U. S. Department of the Interior, Indian Arts and Crafts Board, 1969. 87p. illus., map, bibl. (Native American Arts, 2).

The most complete coverage of the subject, with emphasis on contemporary artists, including engraving on ivory, non-ivory, graphics, book illustration and fine prints, and offering 91 illustrations. Biographical Listing of the Artists, p. 84-86.

Rudenko, Sergei I. *The Ancient Culture of the Bering Sea and the Eskimo Problem.* Transl. by Paul Tolstoy. Toronto, Published for the Arctic Institute of North America by University of Toronto Press [1961]. 186p. illus., maps, bibl. (Anthropology of the North; Translations from Russian Sources, no. 1).

First published in Russian, 1947. Report on an archaeological survey of the Chukchi Peninsula and work at the site of Uwelen where relationships with Alaska and Siberia were found.

Senungetuk, Joseph E. *Give or Take a Century; an Eskimo Chronicle.* San Francisco, Calif., The Indian Historian Press [1971]. 206p. illus. (part col.), map.

Semi-autobiographical plea for Native rights by a well known graphic artist and teacher. The title answers the question, how much longer must we wait? — *Give or Take a Century.* Includes a list of Native Organizations, p. 203-204, and Names You Should Know, p. 205-206.

Shuster, Carl. A survival of the Eurasiatic animal style in modern Alaskan Eskimo art. In *Indian Tribes of Aboriginal America; selected papers of the 29th International Congress of Americanists, 1949,* ed. by Sol Tax. Chicago, Ill., The Uni-

versity of Chicago Press [1952], v. 3, p. 35-45. illus., bibl.

A discussion of possible relationships of the Ipiutak and other Alaskan styles to the Eurasian animal style art, with especial attention to the nucleated circle and eye motif designs.

Sitka, Alaska. Sheldon Jackson Museum. *A Catalogue of the Ethnological Collections in the Sheldon Jackson Museum.* Sitka, Alaska, 1976. 166p. illus. (part col.), bibl.

Text by Erna Gunther with the assistance of Violet Sell. Description and illustration of a major collection of Alaskan material, mostly collected by Sheldon Jackson in the late nineteenth century. Includes Indian and Aleut material. History of Sheldon Jackson Museum, p. 7-10, by Esther Billman. The Eskimo of Western Alaska, p. 87-153, covers objects by material and type with description of manufacture and use. 44 illustrations.

Smoke Signals. *Alaska.* [Washington, D. C.] U. S. Department of the Interior, Indian Arts and Crafts Board, 1966. 42p. illus., map. (Smoke Signals, no. 50-51).

Special issue: *Alaska.* Most of the information came from George Fedoroff of the Indian Arts and Crafts Board staff. Covers the work of the Board in Alaska with Indian and Eskimo artists and students, and offers illustrations of their work. Describes the Designer-Craftsman Training Project in Nome and the Demonstration Workshop conducted in Sitka.

Smoke Signals. *Antler, Bone and Shell.* [Washington, D. C.] U. S. Department of the Interior, Indian Arts and Crafts Board, 1968. 43p. illus. (Smoke Signals, no. 53-54).

Special issue: *Antler, Bone and Shell.* Text of introductory article by Edward Malin. Covers the working of antler, bone and shell by Indian and Eskimo artists and offers illustration of old and contemporary production.

Snodgrass, Jeanne O. *American Indian Painters; a Biographical Directory.* New York, Museum of the American Indian, Heye Foundation, 1968. 269p. (Contributions from the Museum of the American Indian, Heye Foundation, v. 21, pt. 1).

An alphabetic listing of painters giving biographical information, addresses, lists of exhibitions, collections and prizes. Indexed by tribe, with 23 entries for

Eskimo artists. Key to abbreviations constitutes a list of schools, exhibitions and private and public collections.

Spencer, Robert F. *The North Alaskan Eskimo; a Study in Ecology and Society.* Washington, D. C., U. S. Government Printing Office, 1959. 490p. illus., map, bibl. (U. S. Bureau of American Ethnology Bulletin, 171).

Based on work at Point Barrow, Point Hope and the nearby areas in 1952 and 1953. Thorough discussion of traditional life and cultural change. Finds less cultural disruption than expected. Some coverage of craftsmen.

Spencer, Robert F. and Jennings, Jesse D. *The Native Americans; Prehistory and Ethnology of the North American Indians.* New York, Harper & Row [1965]. 539p. illus., maps, bibl.

Chapter IV, Arctic and Sub-Arctic in Native America, by Robert F. Spencer, p. 119-167. Basic introduction to the Eskimo, prehistoric and historic, with illustration and reference to the literature.

Sturtevant, William C. *Handbook of North American Indians,* ed. by William C. Sturtevant. Washington, D. C., Smithsonian Institution, 1976? 20v. illus., maps, bibl. (In preparation).

A proposed monumental work which will probably supersede Hodge's *Handbook of American Indians,* 1907-1910. To be a series of scholarly articles by specialists in encyclopedic form. Volume VI. *Arctic;* Volume XV. *Technology and Visual Arts;* Volume XVII. *Biographical Dictionary.* For a full description see: Sturtevant, William C., Smithsonian plans new Native American handbook, *The Indian Historian,* v. 4, no. 4, 1972: p. 5-8.

Swinton, George. *Sculpture of the Eskimo.* Greenwich, Conn., New York Graphic Society [1972]. 255p. illus. (part col.), maps, bibl.

A well illustrated study covering the entire subject, with emphasis on recent Canadian material. Extensive bibliography on Eskimo art, p. 244-251.

Thule Expedition, 5th, 1921-1924. *Report of the Fifth Thule Expedition, 1921-24, the Danish Expedition to Arctic America in Charge of Knud Rasmussen.* v. 1-10, 1927-1952. Copenhagen, Gyldendalske Boghandel, Nordisk Forlag, 1927-1952. 10v. illus., maps, bibl.

Report of a major expedition from Greenland to Alaska. Popular account given in Rasmussen's Across Arctic America, 1927. Report of the Expedition by Therkel Mathiassen, v. 1, no. 1, 1945. Full contents: I. Report of the Expedition; II. Botany and Zoology; III. Physical Anthropology and Linguistics; IV. Archaeology of the Central Eskimos; X. Archaeology and Ethnology of the Western Eskimos.

Tundra Times, v. 1, no. 1-, 1962-. Fairbanks, Alaska, Eskimo, Indian, Aleut Publishing Co., 1962-

Published weekly on Wednesdays. Native newspaper carrying news items and articles of current interest from a Native point of view. Includes news of art activities.

U. S. Congress. Senate. Committee on Interior and Insular Affairs. Alaska Native Land Claims; Hearings before the Committee on Interior and Insular Affairs, United States Senate, 90th Congress, 2d. Session, on S2906, a Bill to Authorize the Secretary of the Interior to Grant Certain Lands to Alaska Natives. Settle Alaska Native Land Claims, and for Other Purposes, and S1964, S2690, and S2020. Related Bills, February 8, 9, and 10, 1968. 508p.

Complete transcription of statements before the Committee. Includes The Primary issue: ''What Rights to Land Have the Alaskan Natives'', by William L. Hensley (Iŋŋaġruk), p. 66-74.

Van Stone, James W. The autobiography of an Alaskan Eskimo. Arctic, v. 10, 1957: p. 195-210. illus.

Reports on the life of Attungoruk, a Point Hope Eskimo born in 1928, who grew up in a traditional environment and has seen the changes in the life of his people. He now depends on summer employment as well as hunting.

Van Stone, James W. Carved human figurines from St. Lawrence Island. Anthropological Papers of the University of Alaska, v. 2, no. 1; 1953: p. 19-29. illus., bibl.

Description and illustration of a small collection of figurines, including comparison with others.

Van Stone, James W. Eskimos of the Nushagak River; an Ethnographic History. Seattle, Wash., University of Washington Press [1967]. 192p. maps, bibl. (University of Washington Publications in Anthropology, 15).

Based on field work in the area in 1964 and 1965. Not a traditional ethnography, but a study of cultural change. The ivory trade and ivory carving have died out since the nineteenth century.

Van Stone, James W. Masks of the Point Hope Eskimo. Anthropos, v. 63/64; 1968/1969: p. [828]-840. illus., bibl.

Describes and illustrates masks in the collection of the Field Museum of Natural History, Chicago, collected by Miner W. Bruce in 1897 and by John Borden in 1927. The study is based on the author's work at Point Hope in 1967 and on a survey of the literature. 24 illustrations on 8 plates.

Van Stone, James W. Point Hope; an Eskimo Village in Transition. Seattle, Wash., University of Washington Press, 1962. 177p. illus., maps, bibl. (American Ethnological Society Monograph, 35).

Extensive study of a single community covering all aspects of activity. Conclusions; the Village of Tomorrow, p. 158-167, summarizes and offers a prediction of a hopeful future for the village in the modern world. Introduction, p. 3-6 briefly summarizes the ethnological summary of the archaeological and historical past with references to the literature.

Washington, D. C. U. S. National Gallery of Art. The Far North; 2000 years of American Eskimo and Indian Art [by] Henry B. Collins, Frederica de Laguna, Edmund Carpenter [and] Peter Stone. Washington, D. C., 1973. 289p. illus. (part col.), bibl.

Catalog of an important exhibition with 366 illustrations. Eskimo Art [by] Henry B. Collins, p. 1-25, surveys the entire field with emphasis on prehistoric art. Illustrates major pieces from private and public collections.

Waterman, Thomas T. Houses of the Alaskan Eskimo. American Anthropologist, v. 26; 1924: p. 289-292.

A brief discussion of houses and house types of the Western Eskimo and the Aleut.

Webster, Donald H. and Zibell, Wilfred. Inupiat Eskimo Dictionary; illus. by Thelma A. Webster. Fairbanks, Alaska, Summer Institute of Linguistics, Inc. [1970]. 217p. illus.

Basic tool for the language of the Northern Eskimo. Arranged by subject with an English index, p. 186-211. illustrations of some objects are given in line drawings. A Yupik dictionary is in preparation by the Institute.

Weyer, Edward M. The Eskimos; Their Environment and Folkways. New Haven, Conn., Yale University Press, 1932. 491p. illus., maps, bibl.

Based on work with the Stoll-McCracken Arctic Expedition in 1928 and the study of the literature. Long the classic standard work on the Eskimo, covering all aspects in depth, with a stress on environmental factors.

Willey, Gordon R. An Introduction to American Archaeology. Englewood Cliffs, N. J., Prentice-Hall [1966]. 2v. illus., maps. (Prentice-Hall Anthropology Series).

The basic text on the subject. Volume 1, Chapter 7, The Arctic and Subarctic, p. [410]-453, offers complete coverage of the subject and a discussion of differing views, well supported with reference to the bibliography.

Wissler, Clark. Harpoons and Darts in the Stefansson Collection. New York, American Museum of Natural History, 1916. 43p. illus., bibl. (Anthropological Papers of the American Museum of Natural History, v. 14, pt. 2).

A specialized catalog and description with illustrations of the archaeological materials collected on the Stefansson-Anderson Arctic Expedition of the American Museum of Natural History, 1908-1912. The greater part of the material is from the Point Barrow area.

Yupiktak Bista. Does One Way of Life Have To Die So Another Can Live? A report on subsistence and the conservation of the Yup'ik life-style. [Bethel, Alaska, 197-]. 80p. illus., bibl.

Prepared by the staff with the assistance of Art Davidson. ''This report is presented by Yupiktak Bista as a statement on subsistence issues in the Yukon-Kuskokwim Region.'' It offers a discussion and recommendations on public policy issues to find a workable way for the future by maintaining Eskimo values while adapting to the Western world.